Every Place is Holy Ground

Every Place is Holy Ground

Making a pilgrimage through everyday places

Sally Welch

CANTERBURY
PRESS

Norwich

© Sally Welch 2011

First published in 2011 by the Canterbury Press Norwich
Editorial office
13–17 Long Lane,
London, EC1A 9PN, UK

Canterbury Press is an imprint of Hymns Ancient and Modern Ltd
(a registered charity)
13A Hellesdon Park Road, Norwich,
Norfolk, NR6 5DR, UK

www.scm-canterburypress.co.uk

British Library Cataloguing in Publication data

A catalogue record for this book is available
from the British Library

978 1 84825 075 8

Typeset by Regent Typesetting, London
Printed and bound in Great Britain by
CPI Bookmarque, Croydon, Surrey

Contents

To Jeremy, Jess, Si, Ellie
and Binka, with love

Foreword

Sally Welch has produced a wonderfully innovative book to encourage even the most faint-hearted to go on pilgrimage. In one sense she is riding a wave that is already moving fast and gaining speed because pilgrimage has probably never been so popular since the Middle Ages. In another sense she is striking off the well-trodden paths and giving us a new look at an old practice, and for that we must be very grateful.

What Sally does is take us into familiar territory – but territory that we don't know in this context. Through this book we travel round our own spaces – home, church, community – and find that they can actually be sacred places as we look at them with the eyes of pilgrims, entering into those spaces as never before. Sally uses story, symbol, comment, reflection, prayer and much else, wrapping it in a style that is both accessible and profound.

This is a winsome book. It encourages us to leave the deceptive comfort of our chair and enter the more rewarding sphere of pilgrimage. Nothing in pilgrimage is guaranteed except return – and as changed people. Perhaps there is one other thing we can't avoid, and that's adventure, whether of the body, the mind or the spirit. Even if we are taking the route of pilgrimage in our own home we will find that we have travelled far and thought deep. Pilgrimage encourages, challenges, questions, resources and stretches us. We get to know ourselves, our companions, our environment, our values and our goals. And through it all we will also get to know better the Good Companion who travels with us every step of the journey, the Lord of the Pilgrimage, God himself.

So take up your staff, your rucksack and this book – and let's go!

John Pritchard
Bishop of Oxford

PS Sally – thank you!

Introduction

Outside a small stone building a group of travellers is gathering. One by one they emerge from the house, still bleary-eyed with sleep, rubbing their arms for warmth or fastening up their clothes as the chilly morning air hits them. Their breath rises in puffs of white cloud as they exchange brief greetings before turning to adjust their packs, arranging them more comfortably on their backs, checking the fastenings are closed or that the water bottle is easily reached. Then, with one last look round and a final quiet closing of the door, the small party moves off along the path that stretches before them, rough and stony, heavily rutted in some places but clearly marked nevertheless.

As the sun gains in height and strength, the travellers warm up, taking off some outer layers of clothing, relaxing their walking style so that from walking briskly, shoulders hunched and hands thrust into pockets, they become freer, swinging their arms, pointing out interesting objects or parts of the landscape. With additional warmth comes livelier conversation; people start to split off in twos or threes, carrying on animated discussions, striding faster or slower according to their mood or the nature of their discussion. The occasional laughter echoes around the group, bouncing from person to person as comments are snatched up and passed on. The party is joyous now, bunching and spreading out as obstacles such as stiles or deep puddles are encountered and successfully navigated. There is an air of freedom, of holiday, of pure enjoyment in the moment – it feels good to be alive in this place, at this time.

By midday the sun is shining hotly, and the energy and enthusiasm of earlier is starting to wear off. The pace is slower now, the pauses more frequent as individuals stop to gaze at the path ahead, trying to spy out its route as it twists and turns, a pale yellow ribbon edged on either side with fields of green, winding its way up into the dark, blue-green hills in the distance. There are few trees dotted around the landscape, shade is difficult to find, and one by one water bottles are being shaken and tipped upside-down in an effort to catch the last stray drops of liquid from the bottom. Conversation grows more infrequent as energy is conserved for walking, large dark patches of sweat appear from beneath the loaded packs of the walkers, foreheads are mopped, hats removed – and used briefly as fans – before the burning sun necessitates their replacement on the head. The walkers have now drifted apart and are strung along the path like dark beads on a bright gold thread; each preoccupied with their own thoughts, silently trudging, and the route now a harsh taskmaster demanding every ounce of physical and mental strength.

Eventually a large tree provides some welcome shade, and the group gathers together once again, clinging close to the tree trunk, concerned that all should benefit from the respite that its dark-green leaves and thick branches offer from the scorching sun. The last gulps of fluid are shared, bread broken and apples munched – a meagre meal, but thankfully eaten for the day's efforts have been great. Then the walkers stretch out on the ground, heads resting on their bundles, sticks laid out next to them like so many skeletal spouses, voiceless helpmates on the journey. A deep silence hangs over the group, broken occasionally by a snore or a hand slapping against an irritating insect.

Slowly, reluctantly, the first of the walkers stands up, stretches, and looks out from the shade of the tree to the landscape in front.

Far in the distance can be seen the shimmering light which is the sun's heat bouncing off the tiled roofs of the village that is their resting place for the night. With a sigh, burdens are shouldered once more and the group sets off, scarcely refreshed by its slumbers, eager to cover the distance that lies between them and the village.

At last the small collection of houses that for so long has danced just out of reach, seeming to recede along the path as one approached it, becomes a reality. Individual houses can now be made out, and the pace quickens as the end of the day's journey is in sight. Gone is the languor of the early afternoon – a briskness and eagerness now marks the walkers' steps. Small groups of two and three form once more and the sound of conversation is again heard above the crunching of stones along the path. The first few to reach the village square plunge their heads into the trough beneath the drinking fountain, spraying the rest with water, laughing loudly, relieved that they need travel no further that day. The heavy wooden door in the street opposite is marked with a scallop shell, the sign of St James. The large door handle is slowly turned and one by one the walkers enter its promised coolness and are absorbed into the dim spaces of the interior. The door closes behind the last one, its metalwork shining in the sun that has by now lost much of its fierceness, and the village square is silent once more.

This narration of a day's journey on a pilgrimage to Santiago de Compostela, one of the world's great Christian pilgrimage destinations, is as timeless as pilgrimage itself. For nearly 2,000 years people have undertaken a 'spiritual journey to a sacred place'. Inspired by a multiplicity of reasons, following any one of hundreds of the pilgrim routes that criss-cross the United Kingdom and Europe like the silken threads of a gigantic spider's web, hundreds of thousands of people every year seek enlightenment or healing. They walk for rest and relaxation or as a penance, seeking divine aid or in gratitude for help received. In undertaking a pilgrimage we are following a route that has been trodden by many people before us, yet each time it is different. Each individual experiences something unique to him or her and each time valuable personal insights are gained.

Perhaps the original impetus that lay behind the first pilgrimage was the desire of people to see for themselves those places that were read about in the Bible. Actually to stand where Christ had stood, to walk along the Via Dolorosa following in his footsteps as he carried that terrible cross, might, it was felt, bring an added depth and reality to one's faith. Legend has it that St Helena, mother of the Emperor Constantine, who made Christianity the faith of the Roman Empire, travelled to Jerusalem in the year 326 and gathered lots of relics of objects that had been touched or used by Christ and the disciples, bringing them back to Europe with her. From the late fourth century AD we have the first of the written pilgrims' guides, the famous 'peregrinatio egeria'. This takes the form of a letter written by a Gallic woman named Egeria, describing, to a circle of women back home, her journey to the Holy Land. More formalized guides include the Codex Calixtinus written, it is believed, in about 1140, which provides practical information for pilgrims, as well as hymns and prayers for the route. This indicates that by this time pilgrimage must have reached a certain level of popularity for a guide to be thought necessary. By AD 1200, pilgrimage was an important part of European Christian life.

It is difficult, from this distance, to gauge the exact nature of the motivation of people undertaking what was in those early days an extremely difficult and dangerous journey. Probably, as today, there were as many reasons as there were pilgrims. Certainly not everyone's motives were easily definable, but a few main purposes can be identified and, to a large degree, these reasons still hold good today.

Right at the heart of pilgrimage is the idea that some places on this earth are more spiritually significant than others, and that a journey made in seriousness to one of these locations can carry important spiritual benefits. Traditionally, the three most famous pilgrimage sites have been Jerusalem, Rome and Santiago. To visit the places where Jesus lived, stayed, preached and died is of great historical interest, often giving a sense of 'bringing to life' of the Bible. However, other places too were held to be, if not quite as significant as Jerusalem, at least of great importance. Rome had powerful connections with St Peter, made additionally important by the fact that it was the home of the Popes, and Santiago de Compostela in Spain is reputed to be the burial site of the body of St James, which was washed ashore off the Spanish coast. In addition to these three major sites are many hundreds of other secondary places whose sacredness is felt to be greater than that of mere ordinary churches or other buildings. The medieval belief that by travelling to places where saints had lived or performed miracles a closeness was gained to the saint concerned, which perhaps could put one in favour with him, has to a large extent disappeared nowadays. What remains, though often less clearly articulated, is a feeling that some places serve as a bridge between this world and the next, between the reality of earth and the possibility of heaven.

Not all these places needed to be a long distance away. Places such as the island of Iona in Scotland and Holy Island off the Northumbrian coast are long-established pilgrimage destinations, renowned for the holiness of their atmosphere. Other sites too offered pilgrims an opportunity to pray where saints had prayed before them, such as the Shrine at Walsingham, the site where in 1061 Richeldis was told by the Virgin Mary to build a house similar to the one in Nazareth that sheltered the infant Christ; or Canterbury Cathedral, the scene of the murder of St Thomas Becket.

In addition to the experience simply of travelling to a sacred site can be added the desire for healing, either physical or mental or spiritual. Medieval pilgrims would often travel to the shrines of saints who were reputed to have a particular power to heal a specific illness – St Margaret's Well at Binsey near Oxford, for example, would be visited by those suffering from afflictions of the eye. The more severe the illness, the more powerful the saint needed to be and the greater the distance to be travelled. Today, the site of Lourdes, particularly renowned for healing miracles, receives some five million visitors a year, a sure indication that a desire for healing is still a powerful reason for pilgrimage even in the sceptical twenty-first century.

Often, however, the sickness was not physical but mental, engendered by a deep sense of sin, and thus penitential pilgrimages were common. By the eleventh century this concept had become formalized into the notion that forgiveness of sins could be obtained by a formal visit to a particular shrine – there was even a ranking system whereby the more serious the sin, the further away the shrine, with Jerusalem reserved for the most notable crimes. This idea is still valid today, with many people undertaking pilgrimages when they want to turn their lives around, freeing themselves from the various forms of addiction perhaps, or failures at work or unsatisfactory relationships. This type of pilgrimage has even been formalized as part of the Belgian penal system, with a small number of young offenders being 'sentenced' to travel to Santiago by foot as part of their rehabilitation programme.

Perhaps the greatest motivation for pilgrimage, and the one that research indicates is still the strongest reason today for someone embarking on such a strenuous exercise, is that of taking time out from the ordinary concerns and ties of everyday life to engage more thoughtfully and profoundly with one's spirituality and, if Christian, with God. Set apart from the requirements of everyday society, the pilgrim leaves behind the material and psychological burdens that take up so much of our lives, often filling them to the point where reflection on any level, however shallow, is not possible. Freed from material concerns, distanced from the complications of human relationships, liberated from the constraints of earning a living, Christian pilgrims are able to enter more fully into an examination of themselves and their relationship with their Creator. The resulting increase in self-knowledge and awareness of God's power and love can bring immeasurable benefits on the pilgrim's return to 'normal' life at the end of the journey.

But for many of us, making a long journey over challenging terrain is not an option. Tied by work or family commitments, hampered by financial or health constraints, is it still possible to obtain the same spiritual insights experienced by those who are free to spend many days on journeys? The answer for me has been that our God is not only the God of the wide open spaces and the long winding road, but a God who can be found even in the smallest detail, in the most ordinary actions of our everyday life. The most important task for us is to think and act in such a way that we are enabled to see him there. Great insights might emerge on long journeys, but they can also come from any pilgrim journey, however short, undertaken with open hearts and minds, if we are prepared to listen and to look attentively and mindfully. This book sets out to demonstrate that an effective pilgrimage can be undertaken in any setting, even within our own homes, and that the results can be just as powerful and the insights just as significant, as those gained on a more arduous journey through an unfamiliar landscape.

None the less, some action is required. This is not a bedside book – real movement, real travelling, is an integral part of this pilgrimage even if the journey is no more than that of moving from the front door to a chair, from the kitchen sink to a table.

God loves every part of us, our bodies as well as our minds and hearts – we offer all of ourselves to him on these journeys. Action also stimulates the mind, encouraging it to explore our relationship with God more easily and deeply as the fidgety peripheral bits of our attention are distracted by the physical act of walking. Physical movement makes the act of pilgrimage, the prayer of pilgrimage, more intentional, more deliberate. If, as part of this pilgrim reflection, we walk from the font to the altar in our local church, for example, this gives us the opportunity to focus our minds and thoughts on the very heart of our faith.

Above all, pilgrimage offers us the chance to take some time away from the distractions of everyday life and focus more deeply on our relationship with God. Pilgrimage is a state of mind as much as it is a physical journey – we can take the opportunity to cultivate a mindfulness, an awareness of being fully alive in the present moment. Passing slowly through familiar landscapes we have the opportunity to see them again through different eyes – eyes made alert to the signs of God's glory in creation, to the range of blessings to be found in the scenery that surrounds us, to our own needs and the needs of those with whom we share our lives. We can nurture the gift of living in the present, acutely and sensitively aware of our immediate environment, spending time simply being in God's presence, enjoying his company, being surrounded by his love. This book aims to help us cultivate these spiritual gifts.

The journeys offered in this book are through three different landscapes – that of the home, the interior of our local church and the places where we live. They follow the stages of a traditional pilgrimage and also try to engage with some of the issues that pilgrims encounter along the way – the difficulties as well as the discoveries. All three journeys find echoes in the journeys of Christ upon this earth, from the first journey to Bethlehem, through his interaction with different groups of people on his journey to the cross, walking with the disciples on the road to Emmaus after the first Easter day. These journeys of discovery will bring us back to where we started, as many journeys do, but we may no longer be the same people. The journeys end where they started, as we all do; but with a refreshed mind and an enhanced way of seeing, we may discover God where he has always been – right in the midst of the everyday.

How to use this book

The layout of this book follows the traditional route of a pilgrimage, from the beginning of the journey, through various stages of discovery, encountering difficulties on the way, and arriving back at the beginning. Each chapter has four sections. The first section is the Bible passage, which reflects on part of Jesus' earthly journey; the subsequent three sections echo this journey in different locations: the home, the local church and the local community. Three different starting points corresponding with these locations are given and it is easiest first to decide which landscape you will make your pilgrimage through – your home, your church or your community. Then, as you journey on, you simply need to follow that part of the chapter that relates to your chosen location.

It is important to set aside a specific time to undertake this complete journey, either making the whole journey at one time, or undertaking one stage per day. Domestic pilgrimages, like long-distance ones, are most effective if made altogether at one time. It is, of course, possible simply to take one chapter at a time – many people walk to Santiago or Rome in week-long chunks, taking some years to complete the whole. However, it is preferable simply to set aside one or two hours for your journey and allow yourself to experience it fully.

Mindful journeying is a wonderful thing, but demanding also. Try to make sure that you are not pressurized by external time constraints and that you are mentally prepared to focus on your journey. Move slowly, gently, taking time to listen to the sounds of your landscape. Look carefully around you, observing things in a new way, more completely, absorbing the details that so often get overlooked in the hurry of the day.

Reflections are provided at the end of each section. These are simple to do and use ordinary, everyday objects. If you are planning a pilgrimage, try to collect everything you will need before you begin – you might like to put them in a bag or rucksack to carry as you journey. A list of the objects required will be found at the beginning of each chapter.

Try not to be self-conscious, but cultivate self-awareness. Take note of the feelings and emotions that you experience, whether joyful or unpleasant, writing them down if you wish. Explore your relationship with God, allowing him to speak to you through the everyday.

When you have finished, put away your things and allow yourself some time to pause before you take up your ordinary life again. Give yourself time to reflect on what has happened, and allow your insights to change and grow as you meditate upon them. I pray that a new reality will infuse your present one, shining light on the ordinary and filling it with love.

1

Beginning

Scripture reading
Luke 1.5–20, 57–64 – Zechariah and Gabriel

Starting point at home
The front door

Starting point in church
The font

Starting point in the community
Boundaries

What you will need
- *at home* – a stone
- *in church* – an apple
- *in the community* – pen and paper

There is a quote taken from a church on the pilgrimage route to Santiago de Compostela: 'Every journey begins and ends at home'. The beginning of a journey is often harder to define than that, however. Is it when the decision is first made to go on pilgrimage, or when the tickets are booked? Or is it when the front door is finally closed on the first morning of the journey itself? Any of these moments can serve as a beginning, but one thing they all have in common is that they are moments of action. Pilgrimage is a practical exercise as well as a spiritual one – the spirituality can be found in the practicality.

I remember sitting in the harvest assembly of the local church primary school. I had given a talk on 'the sower and the seed' and was listening to the notices. After the obligatory lecture on playground behaviour, the head teacher pointed to the impressive display of canned and dry food that had been donated for the local Food Bank. 'Stand up all those who brought things for the Food Bank,' she said. About a quarter of the children stood up and were given a round of applause. 'Now, hands up all those who thought about giving food but didn't actually get round to it.' A further two-thirds of children raised their hands, eager to receive affirmation for their good intentions. The head teacher looked at them: 'The difference between meaning to do something and actually doing it is the difference between one table of food for hungry people and four tables,' she said sternly. 'It's no good just thinking about it – you must do it too.'

We can talk about pilgrimage, read books, discuss routes, even buy the equipment we believe is necessary, but unless we make that final effort that takes us from the realm of thought to that of action it will be to no purpose. Let us act now and move to the place where our journey will start – the front door, the font, the boundary marker. We will never be completely ready, we will never be totally unafraid, but it is time to step out now: time to begin. So we will start with the first action – the announcement of the birth of John, the closing of the front door, the arrival at the font, standing at the boundary of the community. We will pause, we will reflect and then we will act.

Luke 1.5–20, 57–64 – Zechariah and Gabriel

In the time of Herod king of Judea there was a priest named Zechariah, who belonged to the priestly division of Abijah; his wife Elizabeth was also a descendant of Aaron. Both of them were upright in the sight of God, observing all the Lord's commandments and regulations blamelessly. But they had no children, because Elizabeth was barren; and they were both well on in years. Once when Zechariah's division was on duty and he was serving as priest before God, he was chosen by lot, according to the custom of the priesthood, to go into the temple of the Lord and burn incense. And when the time for the burning of incense came, all the assembled worshippers were praying outside. Then an angel of the Lord appeared to him, standing at the right side of the altar of incense. When Zechariah saw him, he was startled and was gripped with fear. But the angel said to him: 'Do not be afraid, Zechariah; your prayer has been heard. Your wife Elizabeth will bear you a son, and you are to give him the name John. He will be a joy and delight to you, and many will rejoice because of his birth, for he will be great in the sight of the Lord. He is never to take wine or other fermented drink, and he will be filled with the Holy Spirit even from birth. Many of the people of Israel will he bring back to the Lord their God. And he will go on before the Lord, in the spirit and power of Elijah, to turn the hearts of the fathers to their children and the disobedient to the wisdom of the righteous – to make ready a people prepared for the Lord.' Zechariah asked the angel, 'How can I be sure of this? I am an old man and my wife is well along in years.' The angel answered, 'I am Gabriel. I stand in the presence of God, and I have been sent to speak to you and to tell you this good news. And now you will be silent and not able to speak until the day this happens, because you did not believe my words, which will come true at their proper time' . . . When it was time for Elizabeth to have her baby, she gave birth to a son . . . Then they made signs to his father, to find out what he would like to name the child. He asked for a writing tablet, and to everyone's astonishment he wrote, 'His name is John.' Immediately his mouth was opened and his tongue was loosed, and he began to speak, praising God.

Sometimes it is hard to know where a story begins, or where to begin a story. Everyone has a different idea about the beginning of an event, as well as the significance of the details that make up the event itself. For the Gospel writer Matthew, it is important to let us know that Jesus is descended from David; his story begins with the rhythmical recitation of the family tree, then heads directly into the event of Joseph's discovery of Mary's pregnancy. Mark takes a more immediate approach – his account of Jesus' life opens with John the Baptist preaching repentance and preparation; we meet Jesus as a man at the start of his ministry. John heads right back to before the beginning of the world before he, like Mark, introduces us to Jesus through his baptism by John.

Luke's approach is different. The person we first meet is only indirectly involved with Jesus; it relates simply to the father of the man who is to be the herald of Christ's coming. Zechariah is a pretty ordinary man. He is respected because he is a priest in the temple, distinguished because he and his wife come from a long line of priests, but none the less nothing outstanding. They were good people, Zechariah and Elizabeth – Luke tells us not just that they obeyed all God's laws and commandments, but that they lived good lives in God's sight. There was nothing hidden, no furtive sin, no deception or mere show of piety – with Zechariah and Elizabeth, what you saw was what you got and what you saw was good. And this goodness was made more remarkable by the fact that it did not seem as if God had greatly blessed them: they had no children because Elizabeth could not have any, and she and Zechariah were now both very old. What years of sadness they must have experienced, this elderly couple, how much shame because of their failure to produce offspring in a society that measured worth, particularly the worth of a woman, in terms of numbers of sons. But this couple bore their sorrow bravely and continued with their ordinary peaceful lives.

The particular day Luke writes about is special for it has fallen to Zechariah by lot to be the one who burns the incense on the altar. It has been calculated that since every direct descendant of Aaron was a priest there might perhaps have been as many as 20,000 priests serving in the temple. For practical purposes they were divided into sections of 1,000 each, and every section served in the temple for two weeks in the year. The tasks of these priests were allocated by lot – to be chosen was possibly the pinnacle of any priest's life. So here was Zechariah, at last serving in the temple. And to add the impossible to the unusual, an angel appears.

To emphasize not just the unexpected nature of this, but its factual accuracy as well, Luke takes care to tell us exactly where the angel stood – just to the right of the altar. Somehow this detail makes the event both more believable and more astonishing at the same time. The angel reassures Zechariah, then launches into a lyric description of the greatness of the child whose birth he is announcing. But Zechariah cannot take all this in – his mind has stopped at the first sentence: 'God has heard your prayer and your wife Elizabeth will bear you a son.' Zechariah is not a man given to dreaming, and years of disappointment must have accustomed him to the idea that he will never be a father. So he cannot help but exclaim at the angel's proclamation. All those years of careful obedience are defenceless against the miracle that is being proposed. And for this one moment of disbelief he is silenced, not to find his voice again until he reasserts his obedience by giving up his rights to claim his son as part of his family – the child will be called John. At last Zechariah has learnt that to go against an angel is not a wise move!

And so begins the wonderful story, not with pomp and heraldry, but with the ordinary colliding with the extraordinary and being transformed.

Starting point at home – the front door

Whole books have been written on the design and history of the front door. Many careful illustrations and photographs dissect the different components of the front door – the porch or canopy, the door frame, the windows and fan lights, the door furniture and the door itself – charting the changes in design that reflect the changing fashions of the time. The purpose of a front door, however, has always been the same: to fulfil the practical requirements of access (or its prevention) both for people and the various effects of the climate, whether cold, heat or rain. How this purpose has been effected has changed over the years, from the sturdy wood with solid iron nails of Tudor times through the architectural responses to the elegance of the Georgians and the fussiness of the Victorians, arriving at the simpler, more directly functional style of today. There is a huge variety of pattern and style in our communities; a short walk along any road will reveal many differences, even in houses that are ostensibly all the same style and design, such as rows of Victorian terraces or clusters of new buildings on twenty-first-century estates. And this is important; the significance of the front door extends well beyond its function as protection and defence. For the front door can reveal a lot about the occupants of a dwelling; a careful examination can enable one to speculate not just about the level of a person's income, but their personality and priorities – even their level of physical fitness. Filmmakers are well aware of this fact – many times a camera will linger on a front door in order to create atmosphere and expectations that may be either met, surpassed or overturned; shots of dirty neglected porches, cobwebby woodwork and cracked or broken glass lead one to expect unpleasantness of some sort or another, while a cheerful, freshly painted, flower-bedecked entrance suggests a warm welcome and some friendly inhabitants. Not for nothing do estate agents remind prospective vendors to make sure their porches and doors are clean and tidy – first impressions count.

The symbolic significance of the front door is also considerable. The door marks the boundary between public and private, between the outside world, where we may have little control over our environment, and the domestic, where within the boundaries of various practical constraints we can order our objects and activities more to our satisfaction and advantage. The function of the door is not fixed rigidly, however. The difference between public and private life has changed considerably over the centuries, with growing and fading demands for privacy and autonomy, reaching a new level of permeability today with the advent of technology such as Skype and webcams, mobile phone applications and Facebook that can give the wider public more access to the personal and private than has been known since those early times when groups of people lived close together for the purposes of protection and warmth. But for now the concept of an 'Englishman's home is his castle' still, for the most part, holds good. It is true that sometimes the people we must open the door to are not those we want inside our homes; sometimes events outside the home will affect the quality of life within its walls. And yet, the front door can still shut firmly, and we can find comfort in that.

Many journeys begin at a front door: big adventures, small excursions, everyday outings, life-changing experiences. But today it is not with the world that we will engage, but with ourselves and with God. Today it is not the exterior that concerns us, but the interior. Today the journey begins as we close the door behind us and we are within.

Reflection

For a journey of any sort to change us, we must be willing to change and to be changed. Sometimes this process is refreshingly simple, at other times we may find pain and difficulty in growth and development.

After his struggle with the angel, in Genesis 28, Jacob takes the stone that he has used as his pillow and makes an altar of it; he pours oil over it, for, he says: 'surely the Lord was in this place and I was not aware of it'. Look around the area that is just outside your front door and find a stone – it can be small or large, but it should have been taken from nearby. Pick it up and look at it closely. Bits of the stone are very smooth to the touch, other parts are jagged and rough. So in our lives there are parts that are going well and smoothly, and others that cause us pain and distress. We are the same in our dealings with other people – we can be kind and caring at times, but in other company we can seem harsh and cruel.

As you hold the stone in your hands, remember God's loving-kindness to all people. As the stone gradually becomes warmer, allow God to melt the cold hard places in your heart.

Place your stone at the corner of the front door of your home as a reminder to yourself that the Lord is in this place.

Lord God, just as you created Adam and Eve by your
   life-giving breath,
fill me again with your Spirit.
Help me to feel alive to the world and to you,
rejoicing in my place in your creation,
ready to explore it further.

Loving God, fill my heart with the knowledge of your love
and my mind with an awareness of your presence.
Help me to remember in the journey ahead
that I am a container for your grace
and as such that I am precious in your sight.

Starting point in church – the font

In my time as priest I have baptized hundreds of babies, and
each occasion has been unique and joyous. Leaning over the
stone font, holding the hopes and dreams of a family in my arms,
the holiness of the moment of baptism has always made itself
known. I have baptized tiny newborns, sturdy toddlers, and even
whole families, when the demands of small children have meant
that I hear the words: 'We never quite got round to it, vicar – can
you do them as a job lot, please?' I like the baptism to take place
during the normal Sunday service, as a reminder to both the regular church community and the baptism family that we are all
connected, all on the same journey, all sharing the same gift of
grace, offered freely to us with no strings attached. And the font
is where it all starts – the first stage of the journey to the heart of
the matter that is our faith.

Fonts will often be among the oldest objects in a church
– the earliest of them will be the biggest, since they were used
for the total immersion of adults. As baptism moved from total

immersion to the pouring of water over the head, so the bowls of fonts became smaller and were raised on pedestals. Some fonts are seven-sided, symbolizing perfection – God resting on the seventh day of creating, the seven angels blowing trumpets in the Apocalypse in Revelation 8–11. Others are octagonal, halfway between the circle, which is the symbol for God, and the square, the symbol of the earth. So the font is the point where heaven and earth come together. Or the eight sides may represent the seven days of the week and the day of the Second Coming towards which time is proceeding.

Fonts built between the early thirteenth and the mid-seventeenth century may also have covers. In 1236, Archbishop Rich decreed that fonts should have locked covers to stop the baptismal water, blessed annually at Easter, being stolen from the font and used in witchcraft. This cover became unnecessary in 1662 when the new Book of Common Prayer decreed that fresh water should be blessed for each baptism.

Since the rite of baptism is the entry point into the community of the church, part of the service was originally held outside the church in the porch or in the baptistery – a separate part of the church building. However, the new baptism liturgy of 1662 began the service at the font. Its position at the west end of the church, opposite the altar at the east, was believed to be a symbol of a Christian's spiritual journey from baptism to Communion.

For us too, the font becomes the location to begin our journey round the church. It is the place of our acceptance into the family of the church, with all its glories and difficulties, its glimpse of the fellowship of all believers and its day-to-day frictions and disagreements. It is the place where we were first washed clean of all sin and it reminds us that just as the story of Zechariah tells of a man encountering the extraordinary, and being changed for ever, so we have the opportunity to encounter that extraordinary gift of grace again and again until we are transformed.

Reflection

Take your apple and go and stand by the font. Look at it carefully – it is a work of God's creation, and it is beautiful. We are told that there were all kinds of fruit placed in the Garden of Eden and that they were good. This apple reminds us of the gifts of God.

The fruit of the tree of knowledge of good and evil that stood at the centre of the Garden of Eden is traditionally held to be an apple. So it was an apple that became the symbol of Adam and Eve's sin in wishing to be like God. We think of our own faults, the things we have said and done that we should have restrained ourselves from, and the things that we neglected to say and do.

> Gracious God, I have sinned.
> There are many things in my life that I have done
> which I am not proud of.
> There are many ways in which I have wilfully tried
> to destroy the precious creation which is me.
> Sometimes I have deliberately chosen the wrong way;
> sometimes this has been by accident.
> I am sorry, Lord, truly I am.
> I know you will forgive me; you have promised me this.
> Please help me to feel forgiven.

The font at which we are standing reminds us that Jesus came to earth so that we could be forgiven for our sins and for the sins of humankind. Place the apple in the font.

> May I continue on my way cleansed and forgiven,
> a new creation in your sight,
> precious to you and to this created world.
> May I tread the path which I am meant to walk with care
> and with love,

aware that as I journey on,
You, O Lord, journey with me.

Remember to take the apple out of the font when you have finished praying.

Starting point in the community – boundaries

The procession was a strange sight, an anachronism in the midst of a busy urban landscape. A young man walked in front holding a large processional cross, followed by a teenager with a thurible – a container for burning incense – with a small boy trotting beside him, holding a brass 'boat' containing the incense, his worried face showing an awareness of the solemnity of the task he had to perform. Behind these three, a robed choir strode out, followed by three priests in white albs and stoles. Finally, there was a straggle of ordinary people, some slightly embarrassed, others with an interest that looked more anthropological than participative. The singing of the choir, though in tune as always, was a bar or two ahead of the stragglers at the rear of the procession, which added to the slightly anarchic flavour of the event. Prevented by contemporary property law from walking the boundaries – unlike their neighbouring parish, whose procession led boldly in and out of various shops and offices, to the consternation of shoppers and pedestrians – this procession instead kept to pavements and footpaths, pausing almost apologetically at the bridges and buildings that formed the parish boundary. The procession had a sort of hesitant defiance about it, symbolic of a church which acknowledges that while it may no longer hold the central role in the community that it once did, it still retains the right to pray for the soul of every person living within the boundaries so carefully walked around.

It is believed that the custom of asserting the boundaries of a community dates back to Celtic times, when each autumn stones or markers around a community were beaten with sticks to drive out evil spirits and cleanse the land. The Romans followed the same custom – Terminus, the god of boundaries, was honoured annually to ensure fertility of the land and plentiful harvest. By Anglo-Saxon times another dimension had entered into the annual ritual of asking blessing on the land. In a feudal age where border disputes could be frequent and deadly, it was vital to reassert boundaries to prevent the claims of neighbouring communities making inroads into precious land. Having sat uneasily alongside these pagan rituals, the Christian Church finally assimilated beating the bounds into its liturgy in AD 467 when the Bishop of Vienne in France, following a series of calamitous events for the citizens of the town, led a procession around the outskirts asking for God's blessing on the town and its inhabitants.

By the Middle Ages, Rogationtide was fixed to three days before Ascension Day – 40 days after Easter. A procession round the parish boundaries marked out the community and asked a blessing on its inhabitants. The occasionally aggressive treatment of boys and young men in these ceremonies served to reinforce these marks at a time when accurate maps did not exist and community memory was vitally important.

Today we are reminded that wherever we live and whatever our inclination we are part of a parish and as such belong to a community. Whether marked out by traditional boundary stones, place name signs or merely by a change in the speed limit denoting entry to another neighbourhood, we can begin our journey around our community standing by a boundary marker. Linking ourselves with generations of inhabitants, joined by folk memory, we can claim identity with a particular community and pray for its blessing. Place is important to us; it is where we experience God in our lives. Luke gives precise details of where the angel appeared to Zechariah so that we can picture what happened; we too can meet God in places that are familiar to us, transforming our experience, and the place itself.

Reflection

Look for the boundary sign of your community – it may be a traditional parish boundary stone or a cross etched into the side of a building. Or neither of these – it could be your village or town name sign: 'Welcome to . . .' If you feel that even this does not mark the beginning of your community, walk out from your home to the furthest point where you feel your neighbourhood extends and stop there.

Imagine you are a bird hovering above your particular area, using the wind to balance yourself just high enough so that you can take in the whole landscape in one glance. What is your community like? What are the important features in its landscape? What are its characteristics as a neighbourhood?

Let your mind float freely, allowing your thoughts and feelings to wander until you can think of about five words that describe your neighbourhood. Write these down.

Reflect on these words, and how they can have both good and bad connotations. Ask God for a deeper understanding of the people and places you will encounter on your journey.

Lord God, my community is a **busy** one, filled with people and traffic. Help me to find a place to slow down, to look around me and to wonder.

Lord God, my community is a **quiet** one, almost empty at some times of day. Help me to hear your life-giving words through the silence.

Lord God, my community is a **clever** one; learning is a way of life, qualifications the prize. Help me to learn from your creation, not just from books. Help me to value people for who they are, not what they do.

Lord God, my community is a **hardworking** one; physical labour is important. Help me to value all types of work and industry.

Lord God, my community is a **rainbow** one; the people here come from many different countries and speak lots of different languages. Help me to value difference and to see the ways in which we are all the same.

Lord God, my community is a **tightly knit** one; the people who live here have known each other for many years. Help me to appreciate familiarity and to look for signs of growth.

Lord God, my community is a **transient** one; many people only stay here for a year or two. Help me to live as if this moment were all that there is, but that it will last for ever. Let me value the present, while seeing eternity within it.

Lord God, my community is a **stable** one; some members have lived here all their lives. Help me to welcome strangers and to value old friends.

2

Prioritizing

Scripture reading
Luke 2.4–7 – the stable

Starting point at home
Water

Starting point in church
The cross

Starting point in the community
The church building

What you will need
- *at home* – a tap, a bowl
- *in church* – pipe cleaners or straws
- *in the community* – piece of string or wool

The film *St Jacques . . . La Mecque*, directed by Coline Serreau, tells the story of two brothers and a sister who are forced by the stipulations of their mother's will to go on a pilgrimage together if they wish to inherit a share of her money. The three of them form part of a motley group led by an experienced pilgrim guide and the film follows the adventures of this group, explaining the individual motives for pilgrimage and revealing the incidents on the journey itself that eventually transform all their lives. On the first day of the journey the group sets off with a vastly different range of luggage among them, itself indicative of their personalities and approach to life. One of the brothers has no luggage at all – he has simply shown up with no preparation or planning. His life has gone badly wrong, but he wants the money to help his daughter and prove to his ex-wife that he is worth something after all. The other brother is a man crippled by anxieties, desperate to plan for all eventualities in the hope of avoiding disaster. He has packed everything he can think of, the latest equipment, the most sophisticated gadgets. His pack is almost as big as he is and he staggers along at the back of the group, barely keeping up with the others. Finally, in an epiphanic moment at the foot of a hill he ducks behind a rock and unloads a vast amount of stuff. With his load considerably lighter, he can proceed rapidly up the hill to join the others at last.

Pilgrimage is a time for assessing our priorities and getting them in the right order. If one is to walk long distances carrying everything for the journey in one backpack, then only the essentials must be included. Too many things, too much weight, will make the journey so difficult as to endanger its success.

Defining what is essential for our spiritual lives may often be a more difficult matter. How much of our emotional and spiritual energies do we waste on objects, activities and feelings that are inessential! A way must be found of sitting lightly to the unnecessary, of accepting its presence in our lives but refusing to be tied down to it. This could be as minor as not allowing a pressing need to accumulate possessions and material things that will interfere with our main purpose in life, whatever we decide that to be. Money, possessions, status – the acquiring of all these things demands energy, time and focus which would be better directed towards praising God and living in his presence. The acquisition of objects involves fear; with accumulation comes fear of loss and the consequent struggle to retain a grip on what are far from being necessities for our existence. Liberated from the struggles to acquire and the fear of subsequent loss, we can move lightly through the world, unhindered by baggage.

We need not deny ourselves the inessentials; we need only seek to live without being possessed by anything, not allowing material considerations to prevent us going beyond our limits. We must seek to surrender ourselves to the will of God. We need not be afraid of enjoying God's gifts, but we must always bear them lightly and be ready to share them or give them away.

Luke 2.4–7 – the stable

> So Joseph also went up from the town of Nazareth in Galilee to Judea, to Bethlehem the town of David, because he belonged to the house and line of David. He went there to register with Mary, who was pledged to be married to him and was expecting a child. While they were there, the time came for the baby to be born, and she gave birth to her firstborn, a son. She wrapped him in cloths and placed him in a manger, because there was no room for them in the inn.

The distance from Nazareth to Bethlehem is 80 miles, and not easy miles either. Even though Joseph and the heavily pregnant Mary knew what to expect, the journey must have stretched out before them, endless and hazardous, haunted by the fear that the baby would arrive before they reached Bethlehem, compounding the difficulties of the voyage. Fortunately for Mary, that didn't happen, but by the time they reached their destination the baby would have been making its presence felt, increasing Mary's fatigue and apprehension. And then the small town was so busy, people rushing here and there, the noise of their conversations competing with the sounds of the animals as they were fed and watered for the night. There was no room anywhere, no space, and no privacy for a frightened young woman and her anxious husband. So the infant came into the world in a place usually reserved for animals, the humblest shelter of them all. Unnoticed by all but two people, there was no room for him amid the busyness of a society preoccupied with its own thoughts and activities, not stopping to notice the presence of heaven among them.

Jesus came into the world to reset our priorities for us. He reminds us that we don't need much, but that what we do need we cannot and should not live without. In his birth he aligned himself with the poor, the outcast, and the dispossessed – those who have nothing, who have learnt forcibly to live with the bare minimum. He teaches us by his example to strive to free ourselves from all that is unnecessary, all that clutters up our physical, emotional and spiritual lives. So often we run the risk of putting the progress of our spiritual journey in jeopardy as we insist on retaining much that is unnecessary – clinging on to old faith practices, nurturing grudges, adhering to rituals that have long become redundant to our spiritual wellbeing. All these things can impede or even prevent our growth.

As we set off on our journey let us leave behind as much of our spiritual and emotional baggage as we can, keeping the path open for new insights and developments. At the same time, however, we must hold even more tightly to the essentials of our wellbeing, placing them at the forefront of our consciousness, and focusing our efforts on understanding and appreciating them.

Starting point at home – water

Three-quarters of the world's surface is covered by water. The Earth is the only body in the solar system in which water is known to exist in large quantities. It is the only chemical compound that occurs in normal conditions as a solid, a liquid and a gas. It contains both hydrogen and oxygen, which are found in all living and most non-living matter. Excessive variations of water bring disaster in the form of floods and droughts . . .

No one can deny the essential nature of water in our lives; although civilization tries to distance itself from the bare means of survival as much as possible, water is still a significant influence. Our patterns of settlement – the location of our villages, towns and cities – developed from the siting of earliest dwellings near good water supplies. In the United Kingdom, our ability to feed and clothe ourselves more easily began with the abundance of water to power mills for grinding corn and providing the energy to drive the shafts and belts for mechanical processes such as weaving looms.

Drinking water, originally drawn from streams and rivers, was channelled and diverted by digging wells and later laying pipes and creating reservoirs. Today there is a drinking water supply in every home – for most of us, water has receded so far into the background of our lives that it is easy to disregard it completely. Yet its power in our lives occasionally makes itself felt, and the most common causes of disruption to our daily lives are often water-based.

When the floods of July 2007 hit Oxfordshire, I was parish priest to a number of small villages. Together with my small son, whose school was closed, we visited as many of the flood-stricken houses as we could, listening to the experiences of the shocked householders, sharing with them their grief at the damage caused to their homes. Such was the impact of these visits that for weeks afterwards my son would not sleep unless his boots were by the side of his bed, in case further disaster occurred. Similarly, frozen pipes caused by cold weather, or water restrictions occasioned by drought, bring us sharply face to face with our dependence on our water supply.

Christ came into the world in a place and at a time when he would have had only the barest essentials for life, placing himself alongside the poorest and most needy sections of the people. His life demonstrated that we can live richly with little, making sure that we keep only the important things at the forefront of our lives.

Reflection

Find the tap that you use most often in your home. It may be at the kitchen sink or out in the garden, or it may be a bath tap or a shower fitting. Place a bowl beneath it to catch the water for reuse, then turn it on and watch it run.

Think of the work of creation that has gone into the formation of water, its gathering, its cleaning and its arrival out of the tap into your home. Think of the many things you use it for during the day – drinking, cleaning, cooking, washing. Let your gratitude for this miracle pour from you with the energy of water rushing from the tap.

Now turn it off and consider those people for whom water is something that must be struggled for. Think of those who must walk many miles to fetch enough water to survive, or those who are forced to watch the ones they love sicken and die through drinking dirty and infected water. Pray for those working for water-related charities and for those who teach others about health and hygiene.

> Lord God, whose spirit moved over the waters of creation,
> I pray for those whose lives are damaged by lack of water or
>   too much of it,
> for those who struggle to survive.
> I pray for those who are at the mercy of the power of water
> through drought or flood,
> and those who seek to help them.

Think of something that is essential for your spiritual life – it may be a quiet time to pray, it may be a visit to a church service. If you consider that you already make enough time for this activity, rejoice and thank God. If sometimes you are squeezed into neglecting what is essential for your spiritual wellbeing, resolve to find time to fit in one more visit, one more time of prayer, than you currently do. Each positive step, however small, is progress!

Now think of something that gets in the way of what is essential for you. Perhaps you spend too much money on luxuries. Perhaps you eat too much or worry too much about what you look like or who you talk to. Resolve to spend less time on these matters, living lightly to them, and not allowing them to come between you and others, including God.

> Lord, our Living Water,
> help me to remember you at all times of day.
> Help me to realize that you are essential to my existence;
> that without you life is dry and filled with dust.
> Help me to take the time to drink
> at the spring of your refreshing and life-giving waters,
> so that I in my turn may live in a way that gives life to others.

Starting point in church – the cross

Interestingly, the cross was not a symbol for very early Christian worshippers; they preferred to use the anchor, the fish – the word in Greek formed by the first letters of Jesus Christ Son of God, Saviour – or the Chi Rho, the first two letters of the Greek for Christ. This was mainly because the issue of the crucified Christ was still proving a bit of an embarrassment for Christian apologists. It was never easy to explain to non-believers the necessity for Jesus dying as he did. Crucifixion was a shameful death, one perpetrated by Roman conquerors on the worst sort of criminals. There was nothing noble or glorious about it – Jesus had left the world as he came into it, lowly, outcast and despised. However, as time went on and some distance grew between the nature of crucifixion itself and its greater meaning, gradually the cross became appropriated as a fitting symbol for the son of God who gave everything for the people he loved.

Any church, of whatever type, will contain at least one cross. It has become the universal symbol for Christ's saving action in the world – a reminder of his death so that all might live. However, these crosses may take different forms, and consequently have meanings that are slightly different. A plain empty cross can remind us that death has been defeated, that the way lies open for us to follow the same path; it is a symbol of God's triumph, his power and might and, for us, a symbol of hope. A crucifix is the name given to a cross with the figure of Jesus. He may be dressed in robes indicating his kingly and priestly nature, his arms outstretched to bless the onlooker, a reminder that he has defeated the power of the crucifixion and, in so doing, glorifies it. Or the Christ figure may be shown suffering the agonies of death. One can stand before this and imagine the suffering caused by the nails through the wrists and ankles, the pain increasing alternately as the weight is shifted to ease the threat of suffocation

caused by the downward pull of the body in the cruciform position. This cross can remind us of his sacrifice and the true nature
of a love so great that it was prepared to take the suffering of
the entire world upon one set of shoulders. Other cross shapes
can convey other shades of meaning; those with pointed ends
– for example, 'passion' crosses – remind us of the wounds of
Christ, while the Celtic cross incorporates the circle of eternity
into its design. Crosses will be present for different purposes also:
perhaps one on the altar, and one used for carrying in proces-
sions. Finally, if diligent searching proves fruitful there may be
evidence of consecration crosses to be found. Traditionally these
were 12 crosses marked on the inside of the church walls at the
time of its consecration. The crosses were painted on or fixed to
the walls. Dating from apostolic times and still continued today,
the consecration of a church marks it out as somewhere dedicated to the worship and service of God. These crosses, often put
high on the wall of a church, are perhaps the most significant of
all, marking the space within as sacred, as holding something
more than can ordinarily be contained. They are a reminder to us
not only of the greatness of God's love for us through the sacrifice of Christ, but of the triumph of life and love and hope over
all things worldly, up to and including death. More importantly
than that, they mark the way to a greater reality, a deeper, richer
level of life that we can only experience occasionally as through
a glass darkly in this life, but that will be ours in full in the time
to come.

Reflection

St Brigid was a very wise and gifted nun who lived in the fifth
century in Ireland. She founded a convent and a monastery and
was renowned for her care of the poor and the sick.

There is a story that tells of her nursing a sick king of one of the local tribes. As he lay in his bed, wretched with fever, there was little she could do except wipe his brow and watch and wait by his bedside. While she waited she prayed. As she was praying she absentmindedly picked up some of the rushes that were being used as a floor covering in the king's chamber and began to weave a cross out of them. The king, distracted with pain, asked her what she was doing. Brigid told him the story of the life, death and resurrection of Christ and his saving work for all people. As he listened, the king felt his fever leave him, and he became a follower of Christ, as did his tribe, thus ending years of conflict in that region.

This story of Brigid reminds us that it is our role as Christians to keep the story of Christ alive, but also that we can find him in the midst of the most ordinary, everyday objects and actions.

It is possible to weave a cross just as St Brigid did, only using pipe cleaners or drinking straws, not rushes!

First, find a place to sit in the church where you can see a cross that particularly appeals to you. Study it for a while and consider what there is about this cross that speaks to you. How might this quality reflect your spirituality? Is it because it is plain, and mirrors your desire to seek simplicity and straightforwardness? Is it because it is a crucifix, and the image of Christ suffering reminds you of his sacrifice for you?

Once you have found your cross, take out your pipe cleaners. Bend all of them in half. Take the first pipe cleaner and hold it so that the ends are pointing to the left. Hook the next pipe cleaner through the first so that it points down towards you, making sure that they meet where they bend. Hook the third pipe cleaner into the second, but this time so that the points are towards the right. Then add a fourth, pointing upwards. This will be the foundation of the cross, with the four bends of the pipe cleaners interwoven in the middle. Continue to add more pipe cleaners in the same order (with the points facing left, down, right, up) until they are

all used. When you have finished, twist the ends together so that
they stay in place.

Jesus, Son of God,
your cross is bare and plain.
It calls me to a life of simplicity,
stripped of all that is unnecessary,
all that clutters up my life.
Help me to come before you just as I am,
focused solely on you and your call to me.

Jesus, Son of God,
you hang before me,
pouring your life out for me.
Your suffering is intense – I can hardly bear to look at you.
You took the sin of the whole world on your shoulders,
you suffered so that we might live.
The light of your sacrifice throws into harsh relief
all the pettiness of my life,
the small unimportant things I cling on to,
which blur the intensity of your gaze upon me.
Help me to cast off the trivia,
to sort the important and significant
from the merely noisy and distracting,
so that I might see your love through your pain.

Starting point in the community – the church building

Entering into any church today, it is hard not to be reminded
of the many dramas and events that must have taken place in a
building that for so many centuries has played a significant part
in English history. Although the complete hold of the church on

its community has declined, there is still today a feeling that the building remains a significant feature of the community landscape, both physically and spiritually. Physically the church in many villages remains the largest building in the village, and often 'the only communal building apart from the phone box', as one churchwarden recently said to me. Spiritually, however, the impact is even greater, although sometimes undeclared.

The church stands as a symbol of God's presence in and love for the community that surrounds it. Often placed at the centre of a community, it is seen by Christians as a statement of belief in a world of non-belief. By uninterested inhabitants it is seen as a witness to the faith of others, perhaps never needed but available if called upon. For believers, the church building gains much of its sacredness through its association with that which is contained within its walls – the significance of some of the events that occur in church mark out the building as a place where God will be encountered. Often there is an awareness of being part of an unbroken line of worshippers gathered from a community that has soaked a building in prayer, making the building, and those of us who enter it, holy.

The building points beyond itself to God, and this is felt by believers and non-believers alike. Today there are still events for which there is limited physical explanation and so a spiritual one is sought. Rites of passage, birth, marriage and death, when celebrated in one place, endow that place with significance in both community and individual memory. Thus the building becomes the holder, the guardian of a community's story. People whose names are recorded in the baptism and marriage registers surround the building, generations sharing a patch of ground and giving it significance to those whose lives will follow the same course.

We do not need a fine building to be good Christians – Jesus demonstrated this by being born in the humblest of dwellings.

But we can honour the place where so many have gathered to mark the important occasions of their lives with prayer.

Reflection

Stand at the front door of the church building in your community. The porch is designed not only to welcome people to the church but to send the congregation out into the world, reaching out in love to the community beyond the church.

Walk slowly round the outside of the building, if you are able. Reflect on the hundreds of significant events that have taken place within the walls. Remember the lives that have been affected by what has happened here – families rejoicing at the birth of a child, two people pledging themselves to each other for their whole lives, a community gathered to mourn the loss of someone they loved. Think of the prayers that have been said in the building, the hopes and fears, the dreams and the terrors that have been voiced, soaking the place in prayer until the whole building becomes a prayer in itself, a monument to a community.

See how large the building is, standing out among the buildings that surround it. Remember that everyone in the community belongs to that church, whatever their particular beliefs or lack of them.

If your church has a graveyard attached to it, walk among the gravestones, pausing every now and then to read the names and dates that are carved on them. All of these stones represent people like us, who lived and died, who knew the same joys and sorrows as we do. Think of the unbroken line of worshippers in this church, and the great love God has shown for us all throughout time.

Eternal God, we have built altars to you, and buildings in
    which to worship you.
Although you are too great to be contained by wood and
    stone,
help us to cherish these places,
to recognize the sacredness of a space
where so many emotions have been shared with you and with
    our community.
Let this building be a sign of your love in this place,
just as we ask you to let our actions to reflect your love also.

'Clypping the church' is based on an Anglo-Saxon practice, which
was revived in the 1800s. Clypping means to clasp or tightly grip;
people would express their love for their house of worship by
forming a circle and walking round the building holding hands.
It was a symbolic act of friendship and love.

Take out your string or wool and examine it. It is made of lots
of thinner threads twisted tightly together. Singly these threads
are weak and insubstantial; together they form a bond of strength
that can be used for all sorts of things. Pray that this community
may become strong together.

Lord God,
You know that we were not meant to live alone,
that we are dependent on each other and on you.
Help us to work together for your purposes
so that we may become strong in your love.

Tie the string at the ends so that it forms a circle. The circle
reminds us of God's unbroken love for us, his Church and for
all his people. Imagine that with this string you are tying a ribbon round the whole church building – 'clypping' it: embracing
it with God's loving care.

Loving God, we pray for the life of our church.
You call us to worship and to service,
to love and to care.
We are a family, united by a common bond of love for you.
Fill us with your grace so that we might serve you better,
an example of love in this community.

3

Discovering

Scripture reading
Luke 5.36–37

Starting point at home
Media: books/newspapers/television

Starting point in church
Pulpit or lectern

Starting point in the community
School or place of learning

What you will need
- *at home* – a newspaper or a storyline from a television soap
- *in church* – ideally a children's Bible, but an ordinary one if not
- *in the community* – a plant seed or a piece of a plant

Evenings can be very long in pilgrim hostels. Physically exhausted by the day's journey, there is little point in going to bed too early; what sleep there is to be found in a large dormitory filled with an assortment of people from all kinds of countries will doubtless be broken by the not so careful tiptoeing and stumbling of pilgrims coming in later to sleep, the rustling of their backpacks and the muted crash of equipment defying all but the most catatonic to find rest. So after the laundry has been washed, the postcards written and the journals filled in, the stories begin. Most people's life stories are too complex to be shared – some may be too troubled to offload lightly on to a passing stranger – so the tales tend to be of events along the road, which is after all the one thing that binds us all together. Experiences of good and bad hospitality are exchanged, horror stories of encounters with dogs or hostile villagers are exclaimed over, and the scars from injuries incurred through river crossings, falls or cooking accidents are displayed. Tales of places and people further up the road are cautiously revealed, the teller aware that these, although they may be little more than hearsay, might offer some degree of preparedness for the days ahead, a state of readiness that has proved more than once to be helpful when encountering savage dogs or farmers angry at the number of walkers across their land. These are the stories that bind the community together, gaining significance in the telling, bringing a sense of fellowship to an undertaking that can be a very solitary and isolating one. It is tales of others' adventures and incidents that can help pilgrims continue when the journey is difficult, aware that others too have faltered yet kept going, often suffering greater setbacks and larger obstacles. And one's own journey in turn becomes the material for new stories, more contributions to the folklore of the pilgrimage, bringing people together and providing a larger meaning than one story alone can bring.

Human beings are storytellers. From the moment the first isolated people gathered together in community for company and protection and found a language with which to express their common needs and desires, stories have played a vital part in growing and maturing that community. Stories were the way to understanding where we had come from and a way of pointing where the community would like to go. They had to be memorable, for stories were around for many thousands of years before they were written down, so they were larger than life, full of characters and action. Stories articulated the terrors of the darkness, giving voice to them and then driving them away. Stories nurtured common purpose and reflected a common past.

In our modern Western world, we have lost touch with a lot of our story. There are so many different stories being told, so many different interpretations and understandings of the world, that we are in danger of being overwhelmed by it all; but as Christians there is one story that unites us all, binds us together with a common memory and a common purpose. It is vitally important that we look for this story in our daily lives, searching for the meaning that lies behind the events that occur, and finding it when we set these events, the happenings, alongside that most great world-changing event that is the Christian story.

But it is not enough to be merely passive listeners to the story. Great stories do not simply flow in one direction, from teller to listener. Great stories are not solid edifices, they are fluid structures, constantly changing and developing in response to situations and circumstances around them. They are in dialogue with the world they reflect and seek to draw meaning from and add meaning to the events of the time. While the kernel of the story – its deep meaning – may remain unchanged, different aspects grow or diminish in importance, with different characters acquiring greater or lesser meaning.

And what of us, we who have taken the Christian story as the one that provides us with the fundamental purpose and meaning for our lives? We are listeners to the story, yes, but to make it come truly alive, to allow it fully to grow and develop and change our every action with a deeper, greater meaning, we must be tellers of the story too. 'But the one who received the seed that fell on good soil is the man who hears the word and understands it. He produces a crop, yielding a hundred, sixty or thirty times what was sown' (Matthew 13.23).

Luke 5.36–37 – new wine

No one tears a patch from a new garment and sews it on an old one. If he does, he will have torn the new garment, and the patch from the new will not match the old. And no-one pours new wine into old wineskins. If he does, the new wine will burst the skins, the wine will run out and the wineskins will be ruined.

Jesus is known to be a great storyteller, and it is this that has helped spread the Christian story as far as it has. Instead of simply telling the facts in a dry, straightforward way, Jesus makes values and truths come alive by embedding them deep in a narrative of everyday life. He uses images and metaphors that are universally known; he takes common situations that everyone encounters – ungrateful children, looking for lost things, turning up late for appointments – and helps us look beyond the outward appearance to find the spark of life, the seed of truth that lies buried within the story. This in turn is transplanted into our own hearts when we make the story our own. But it is not enough simply to listen to the story that Jesus tells; we must absorb it, we must be prepared to be changed.

One of the earliest parables that Jesus tells is about this very condition, and he uses two of the most common things of life to tell us – clothes and drink. Who would, in order to mend an old item of clothing, cut up a new garment to provide the patch? In Jesus' times, garments were made of natural fibres, such as linen or wool, which react in a very strong way to washing, mostly by shrinking. After they have been washed a few times, this reaction settles down and the item is unlikely to shrink more, but the difference between an unwashed piece of cloth and one that has been washed a few times is very striking. In this way, the two garments would be ruined – the new because it had a piece cut out of it and the old because if you attach a new piece of material to an old one, the first time you wash it the new patch will change and shrink in such a way that it will come away from the old fabric, probably tearing the stitching as it does so, thus leaving the old garment in an even worse state. What Jesus means here is that there is little use in trying to take the new meaning that Christianity brings to the world and using it as a patch to fix the holes in our old way of thinking. It is not possible simply to pick and choose the bits of Christianity that appeal to us most and then simply use them to plaster over the bits of our home-grown ideas and philosophy gathered from all sorts of sources that do not hang together. Christianity is a whole new garment, a whole new way of thinking, of seeing, of hearing.

Again, Jesus talks of putting new wine in old wineskins. This is harder for today's listeners to understand – after all, we use bottles or wine boxes, not 'skins'. But in Jesus' time, glass or ceramic bottles were rare, and even clay bottles or jars were owned only by the wealthier members of a community. Ordinary people would make vessels for liquids out of goatskins, and this is what they used for wine. A new goatskin would be taken, soft and flexible, and freshly made wine poured into the skin, that would then be left to ferment. The fermenting process released gases that would expand the new, flexible goatskin. Once the wine was fully fermented it was ready for use. The goatskin, when it was empty, could not be used again, as the fermenting process had stretched the skin as far as it would go – any more fermenting and the skin, stretched and brittle with age, would split open, spilling the wine. Jesus reminds us here that we must not try to make the new thoughts and beliefs of Christianity, the new way of thinking and seeing, fit in with our old, human ways. Our minds need to be flexible, able to stretch and grow with the demands of thinking and loving in the new way. The process might not be pain free – accommodating the new often isn't – but there is no way that a worldly, selfish style of thinking can be incorporated into a life lived fully in Christ.

The stories Jesus tells, his parables, are not easy to understand. He did not mean them to be. They are stories that are grounded in reality, in everyday experience, but that point beyond the every-day to the eternal, making us think and act in new and different ways – ways that are often difficult and certainly uncomfortable. They demand new ways of thinking and looking at the world, and we may never be fully reconciled to all their meaning. They ask for active engagement, dynamic interaction, puzzling dialogue. They intrigue, they challenge, and they demand us to be differ-ent. And these stories, when taken and studied and discussed and lived, can certainly change us.

Starting point at home – media: books/newspapers/ television

'Bang! And the dirt is gone!' our two-year-old son joyfully exclaimed whenever we went into the kitchen. My husband and I could not understand what he was talking about; it was his first real sentence, somewhat later than average, and it made no sense at all! Bang – what was that? Some sort of reaction to doors slamming, perhaps, a common occurrence in our noisy household? And what was all this preoccupation with dirt? We couldn't think what he was talking about. And then one of his older siblings enlightened us – he was quoting the catchphrase for a cleaning product that had been advertised on television. All our careful educating, diligent singing of songs, reading stories, obsessively limiting his access to appropriate television, and what had captured his imagination was a slogan from an advert watched while he was being babysat by his big brother!

It is now such a truism as to be hardly worth stating that we are bombarded by all sorts of messages through all sorts of media. Television, newspapers, magazines and books provide a multitude of windows on to the world, all looking out on to slightly different aspects, all with their own particular view. And the internet has provided an even vaster outlook, like one of those huge cathedral stained-glass windows, each fragment of glass letting in a different-coloured light, subtly altered by the defects in the glass, the bubbles and the variations in textures. This window allows the world to look in on us as well, perhaps more than we realize, and with the same distortions that we see when looking out.

Our world is trying to tell us hundreds of thousands of stories, to impress upon us many different viewpoints and attitudes. It would be easy to lose one's way through them all, to wander in a confused state among the opinions and beliefs on offer, attracted first to one then to another, depending on which one is shouting the loudest. Easier too to pick and choose which bits of the stories on offer are most attractive and to collect only these, sticking them together in an attempt to provide a personalized way that is easy to live with and through, that provides a justification for our less attractive character traits or allows us to continue with damaging behaviour patterns. The other extreme, however, is not recommended either. Finding one story and sticking to it dogmatically, not allowing the changing world to impact at all upon our inner selves, closes the door to change and growth, to transformation and new directions. We need to listen to the stories of the world and then reflect on them through the lens of Christ, using the Christian viewpoint to understand and criticize, to enhance and learn from. One-way conversations are never satisfactory; a dialogue between our inner selves and the outside world, mediated through the value and beliefs of that first great Word, will bring insight and understanding to both sides of the conversations. Just as it was impossible to protect our son from the ubiquitous reach of the advertising slogan, so it is impossible to live in the world without engaging with it. What is needed is a story, an overarching narrative that can enable us to engage critically with the outside world and gain new understanding from this engagement.

Reflection

Look through your newspaper or a magazine. Find a story that strikes you as interesting, that resonates with you for whatever reason. Read it through again slowly and carefully. What is the message it is giving, and what is the viewpoint of the person who has written the article?

If you can, think of a parable that Christ told that either reflects or contradicts the message behind your story. How does this help us to understand the characters better? How would you react in this situation – in a way that fits in with the world or the gospel?

Try the same thing with a storyline from a soap on the television. Does this change the way you view the characters and their actions?

Starting point in church – pulpit or lectern

One of my favourite stories in the Bible occurs in the book of Nehemiah. It is not a very big story and not very much happens, but it is all about story and the value of storytelling. The Israelites are in trouble. Centuries earlier, God had given them some amazing gifts – a promise and a country – and these things brought wonderful prosperity with them. This promise and this country were what bound the Israelites to God, keeping them reliant on him and responsive to him. As the years went by it seemed that whatever the Israelites did, or did not do, they would prosper. But they were wrong. The Israelites ended up being driven out of their country and exiled to Babylonia. By the time they returned to their homeland they had forgotten much of their religion. It seemed that their country had forgotten them – the walls of Jerusalem were nothing but rubble and the great temple was just a heap of stones.

With a great surge of energy, led by Nehemiah, the Israelites laboured long and hard to rebuild their city. When the work was finished, everyone gathered in the main square. The new walls round the city gave them security and the new temple a place to worship, but they were still at risk from enemies and internal divisions. They needed guidance and reassurance. So Ezra, the priest, fetched one of the scrolls on which the sacred texts were written and he began to read from the Pentateuch – the first five books of the Bible. These stories needed to be translated into a language that could be understood, so 13 priests walked among the people, interpreting and explaining the stories to the Israelites so that the meaning became clear for all.

As Ezra read those great stories of Noah and the Ark, of Abraham and God's promise to him, of Joseph and his spectacular coat, of Moses and the Exodus, a wonderful thing happened. Those wandering Israelites, returned from exile but not feeling at home, recognized themselves in the stories they heard. They remembered their God and his great love for them and they experienced again what it meant to be one of God's people. Initially torn with shame and loss, they were told by Ezra not to mourn the fact that they had been lost but to rejoice in the fact that they were found again, and celebrate with feasting.

The pulpit and lectern stand traditionally between the altar and the body of the congregation, the nave. Its position is symbolic – those who stand up at the pulpit and the lectern are mediating the word of God, the stories of God, to the congregation. Just as in the story of Nehemiah the reader and preacher translate the events of the story into language, thoughts and ideas that bring to life the meaning behind the story, the lectern traditionally stands surrounded by the four evangelists – the writers of the Gospels, the story of Jesus. Very often the part of the lectern that supports the book is in the shape of an eagle; the Bible rests upon the outstretched wings of, traditionally the only creature that can gaze directly into the eyes of God. It reminds us of the power and importance of the Bible – the truths it contains, the life it proclaims, and the challenges it offers.

The pulpit too is designed to remind both us and the preacher of the importance of the task that they undertake. Just as the 13 priests worked among the people, translating and interpreting the sacred text to the Israelites, so do we need people to meditate and reflect on the word of God and share with us the results of these reflections. We, as the people of God, gather together to hear the stories of God, to think about them, to discuss them, and then to allow the results of those discussions to change the way we think and interact with the world.

Reflection

To do this reflection it is best if you can lay your hands on a children's Bible. These have the main stories of the Old and New Testament in clear, simple language, often with illustrations. If you cannot find one of these, then try to find a Bible that has headings for each new story.

If you have a pulpit or a lectern in your church go and sit at its foot, on the steps if they have steps, on the floor if they don't. As you sit, leaf through the Bible, looking at the pictures and reminding yourself of the stories that are within it. Allow yourself to marvel at the huge variety of experiences that are recounted within the book – tales of great courage and great treachery, of bitter sorrow and huge joy.

Pick a story that speaks to you particularly at this time and in this place, and read it slowly, savouring the details and listening to what it says to you.

The statutes of the LORD are trustworthy, making wise the simple. (Psalm 19.7)

[God's laws] are sweeter than honey, than honey from the comb. (Psalm 19.10)

Open my eyes so that I may see wonderful things in your law. (Psalm 119.18)

Your word is a lamp to my feet and a light for my path. (Psalm 119.105)

Take the helmet of salvation and the sword of the Spirit, which is the word of God. (Ephesians 6.17)

All Scripture is God-breathed and is useful for teaching, rebuking, correcting and training in righteousness. (2 Timothy 3.16)

But the man who looks intently into the perfect law that gives freedom, and continues to do this, not forgetting what he has heard, but doing it – he will be blessed in what he does. (James 1.25)

Starting point in the community – school or place of learning

Having recently moved from my post as rector in a rural benefice, I was reflecting on what I had learnt and experienced during the four years in which I had been privileged to serve my communities. I learnt a huge amount about many things, but I was surprised to realize that the area in which I had learnt the most had happened quite without my noticing, and that much of my spiritual growth had come about through a group of schoolchildren.

There were three schools in my benefice – two Church of England primary schools and one independent preparatory school – and I was a regular visitor at all of them, leading assemblies, conducting services, and showing various classes round the churches in the benefice. Originally my assemblies were based on the Core Values used in teaching; topics such as Integrity, Friendship and Loyalty were the subject of the week or month and my assemblies looked at Bible stories that highlighted these values. However, after consultation with the head teachers, it was decided that I should concentrate simply on telling some of the classic Bible stories that were an essential part not only of a child's Christian spiritual development, but of their British cultural understanding as well – after all, references to the 'judgement of Solomon' are lost if there is no knowledge of that story.

Accordingly, I began at the beginning, with Adam and Eve, and started to work my way chronologically through the Old Testament. Every fortnight I told a story and then reflected on its message for us today as Christians. As time went by I got into my stride and my stories became more dramatic, and my subjects more adventurous. They also became more challenging for me; what is the Christian message implicit in the story of Jacob's deception of Esau, and how can we apply what we learn from this story to our lives today? Things became more interesting still when we arrived at the lesser known stories of the Bible, particularly the activities of the Old Testament prophets. What a strange group of people they were, scattered throughout the time covered by the Old Testament. Taken from different types of people in a mixture of situations, it seemed at first as if there was little linking them apart from their title. And yet here they were, chosen by God and appointed, sometimes willingly, sometimes not, to speak on his behalf in various locations to motley groups of people who chose either to listen or to ignore the words of the particular prophet assigned to them. These characters lived lives full of incident and, since what they said was often not popular, full of danger as well. Often possessing flaws themselves (consider Balaam and his habit of expecting payment for his prophecies and Jonah's temper when the people he prophesies to actually do repent), they were none the less charged with relaying the messages of God to his chosen people.

Interestingly, these messages were not original; the prophet's job, in the main, was not to give new insights or relay new commandments, but to call God's people back to their original relationship with him as laid down in the Mosaic covenant. The prophets reminded them of the blessings and curses of this relationship, its uniqueness and its preciousness. They were not reformers or radicals; they attacked only crimes against the covenant and sought always to bring people back to God, however far away they had strayed.

As I related the stories of Balaam and of Deborah, of Jeremiah and Miriam, this simplicity of purpose became ever clearer. And just as clear was the single outstanding message that I shared week after week with the schoolchildren. Every story told of the frailty of human beings: their flaws, and their habit of doing the wrong thing whenever the opportunity presented itself. Equally, every story told of the majestic nature of God's people when they rose to the challenges that God put before them: the wonderful things that were accomplished in his name for the good of his people. And every story told of the never-failing love of God for his fragile, damaged children, who constantly strayed from the covenant relationship, testing it to its limits and beyond, incurring God's anger and punishment on occasions, yet never cutting themselves off completely from his forgiveness and grace.

Reflection

Walk to your nearest school or college. If there are none in your community, find a building where teaching takes place – it may be a community hall or scout hut or even a pub that hosts a reading group. Education is so often cited in the media as a problem or as a political issue, it is easy to forget what a great privilege it is to have access to education and possibilities for learning so plentifully available.

Look around you and see if you can find a seed from a tree or a plant. If you cannot find one, find anything that is green and living! Think how this seed that is now so small will grow and become mature; how it will be a thing of beauty and of usefulness, how it will become part of God's glory.

I hold in my hand a seed.
I am not sure what it will become –
a flower, a shrub, something colourful or something green.

What I do know is that God's glory will shine through it.
For the whole of God's love for his creation
is contained in this seed.
And I hold it in my hand.

Children, too, hold all their potential inside them. They can grow
tall and strong, nurtured by love and freed to become their true
selves, or they can be damaged and bent out of shape. Pray for
all who learn in this building that they may grow to reflect God's
glory in their lives and actions, able to realize their potential. Pray
for yourself that you may never let go of the capacity to learn.

4

Struggling

Scripture reading
Luke 29.39–44 – Gethsemane and after

Starting point at home
Shoes

Starting point in church
Candles

Starting point in the community
Hospital/doctors' surgery

What you will need
- *at home* – the shoes you are wearing
- *in church* – a candle (and something to light it with)
- *in the community* – a stick

We had arrived in Assisi the afternoon before. Excitedly we had walked around the small town just as the shops and businesses were closing and the restaurants and cafés filling up for the evening. We had eaten our first meal in Italy and slept somewhat erratically in the small room that only accommodated the six of us if those who did not share a bed slept on the floor. Now, however, it was the first morning of our pilgrimage. We stood at the town gate for the obligatory photograph and could see the pilgrim path stretching out before us, winding down the hill, across the valley and then disappearing into the wooded slopes of another hill. Our kit was clean, our hearts were full, our spirits high.

As we strode off down the hill it began to spot with rain. By the time we reached the bottom of the hill it was raining in earnest. After an hour we were cold and wet. By lunchtime we had had enough of the whole journey and if the road back had not been quite so steep we would have turned round there and then. By the time we reached the place where we were staying we had added fatigue and hunger to our list of woes. Added to this, the hotel was cold, the water supply inadequate, and the food frankly horrible. That night we pushed all the beds together and huddled up for company and warmth, gaining comfort from the presence of each other, chatting quietly in the dark until one by one we fell asleep.

Fortunately for us the next morning brought bright sunshine, a fantastic breakfast and a gentle walk along a valley, but the memory of that first day and night is still a reference point in the family for an event that requires all one's reserves of fortitude and perseverance!

Any pilgrimage or journey will contain within it elements that are difficult. Physical problems such as blisters or sore muscles can make progress very slow and painful, and this is often made worse by the shame of seeing former companions of our journey walk on past us, going so much faster than we can. External conditions, such as bad weather or a rough and stony track, or the dreariness of walking along a busy road, can make the journey seem very tedious and that night's resting place a long way away. At times such as these it may seem as if the whole enterprise is a bad one and the best thing to do is give up and go home.

We all have different methods for dealing with such occasions, but one of the most important things to realize is that we are not alone. Those people for whom life seems to be going so well, for whom the journey appears so lighthearted and easy, they too have found the road to be a hard and unforgiving taskmaster at times. Maybe even now they are suffering, masking their pain for their own sake or for the sake of others – perhaps because there is no one with whom they can share what they are going through.

Luke 22.39–44 – Gethsemane and after

Jesus went out as usual to the Mount of Olives, and his disciples followed him. On reaching the place, he said to them, 'Pray that you will not fall into temptation.' He withdrew about a stone's throw beyond them, knelt down and prayed, 'Father, if you are willing, take this cup from me; yet not my will, but yours be done.' An angel from heaven appeared to him and strengthened him. And being in anguish, he prayed more earnestly, and his sweat was like drops of blood falling to the ground.

This short extract is one of the most important parts of the story of Christ's life on earth. Jesus is looking towards death, but he is afraid. He has just eaten his last meal with these friends who loved him but could not understand him. Still less could they walk alongside him on his journey now – he knew he had to do this alone.

Space was at a premium in Jerusalem, busy and crowded at all times of the day and night; it was difficult to find anywhere to go where he could have some peace and quiet. There were few private spaces in Jerusalem but some rich people had gardens on the Mount of Olives and it was into one of these gardens that Jesus went, driven by his restless fear to seek comfort from God. He was only 33 – no one wants to die at such a young age. He knew the task that lay ahead of him and he did not want to undertake it – he was truly afraid. Jesus entered the garden frightened and alone and sought help from the only one who would give it to him. And he prayed intensely, so intensely that the effort was wringing sweat from him. And first he prayed the prayer of a frightened man: 'Don't let this thing happen to me, God, I don't think I can bear it.' But he continued to pray and to struggle until finally he could pray the prayer of a trusting man: 'Your will, not mine, be done.' This was not the prayer of a defeated man, who had fought and lost and now saw the ending of his hopes and dreams in terror and pain. It was the prayer of a man who was trusting in God his Father to love him with a perfect love even if the ways of this love seemed difficult and strange.

Jesus left the garden a transformed man. He had put aside his fear and, in an act of perfect submission, also put aside his own will to take on that of God wherever that might lead him.

So too must our prayers be, however difficult this seems. We must try not to give God a list of our requests, suggestions for how he might make life easier or better for us. We must endeavour instead to ask for trust in a perfect love that will never let us go, so that we can say the words of Julian of Norwich: 'All shall be well and all shall be well and all manner of things shall be well.'

Starting point at home – shoes

I was working with a group of children and their teachers in a primary school. The children were in their last term at the school, moving on to secondary school in September, and I was exploring with them the idea of journeying. We decided we would make a small labyrinth out of our shoes. A labyrinth is a single path that takes a winding, circuitous route to a centre point where the traveller can reflect for a while before taking the same path out. It can be used as a metaphor for life's journey, and walking it can help us reflect on where we are now and where we are going.

The children and the teachers all took off their shoes and we arranged them so that they formed the outline of the labyrinth, lining the path the children were to walk. The children then walked the labyrinth, reflecting on their time at their current school and their hopes for their new one.

The exercise worked well, and the children soon seemed absorbed in their thoughts. I too was reflecting, but on a different matter. The sight of all those shoes laid out made me think about the stories that each shoe held about the owner and the path he or she trod. There was a pair of shoes worn by a child who loved to play football – the top of the shoe was scuffed from constant contact with a ball. I could see a pair of shoes that although old and worn had none the less been carefully polished by a loving parent that morning. One of the teachers was waiting for a hip replacement and walked with great pain – I could clearly tell her shoes as they were worn down on one side to accommodate the owner's limping gait. Another pair of shoes was brand new and somewhat incongruous in a school setting – bright red and not a little impractical. I knew the owner of these shoes was struggling with a broken marriage and the prospect of much upheaval. Without their owners, the shoes stood as if abandoned, silently speaking of where they had walked and what they had encountered.

Originally designed simply as protection against the weather and rough pathways, it was not long before shoes made other statements about income and status, as well as being formed for the practical needs of the owner. Today, as with much of what we wear, our shoes reflect our personalities and our attitudes to our lives and the issues we encounter. They tell the tales of practical requirements, the need to walk long distances, perhaps, or secret aspirations to a different life, where struggling and difficulties play no part.

Sometimes our lives and behaviour also reflect our inner struggles in ways that are not always attractive. We may become twisted and bent out of shape, reflecting in our behaviour to others ways in which we have been hurt or damaged in the past. Accepting God's will for our lives, determining to follow faithfully his path and walk in his ways, believing always that these ways are good, can be the greatest struggle of all. But if we kneel with Christ and pray for the grace to say, 'Your will, not mine, be done', we too will leave our Gethsemanes transformed.

Reflection

Look at the shoes you are wearing at the moment. Consider why you bought them. What was their purpose? Did you buy them for comfort or for how they looked? Do your shoes reflect your lifestyle or your aspirations, or perhaps a bit of both?

Look at the way your shoes have accommodated themselves to your feet, the places where the leather has stretched over a toe, perhaps, or the buckle has had to be tightened, a heel padded. What sort of accommodations have you had to make in your life? Are there places where you have had to be stretched or tied in? Perhaps an ill relative has meant that you were not free to live where you chose; perhaps an unsympathetic manager has prevented you from enjoying your work as much as you would like. Perhaps your own health has limited the choices you have been able to make in your life.

> Lord, sometimes the steps we can make on this journey
> are very small and painful,
> restricted by our limitations both physical and mental,
> and those of others.
> Help us to be aware of your presence supporting us and
> protecting us, accompanying us as we progress,
> ever so slowly, along the way.

Now take off your shoes and look at your feet. They too bear the marks of our lives. Defenceless and vulnerable, we stand before God. We have taken off our shoes as we are commanded, because we stand on holy ground. Everywhere is holy ground – God created it, he cherishes it, and we can find him there.

> Creator God, I surrender.
> I give up my struggles, my difficulties,
> my pain and my loneliness.
> I give up my habit of clutching these things to me,
> not allowing you to carry the burden of them for me.
> I let go of my lack of faith in you.
> I accept the loving plans you have for me.
> I stand before you, on your holy ground,
> and place myself in your hands.

Starting point in church – a candle (and something to light it with)

The church where I am working at the moment has as one of its focal points an enormous candelabra, hanging from a chain of great length attached to a beam just where the chancel meets the nave over the nave altar. I cannot decide whether it is a thing of beauty or not; certainly it is very striking – it is made of brass, now gently discoloured, and its 12 arms curl out from a central column that ends in a large ball. This design is copied in the two smaller candelabra that hang above the steps to the sanctuary, each also holding 12 candles. These candles are slender affairs and burn down quite quickly, so every couple of weeks the sacristan commandeers a ladder and a helper and goes through the process of changing 36 candles. The church's candle bill is correspondingly high. The effort involved in looking after the candles is not insignificant, but every Sunday, just before the main service, they are all lit and remain lit until the end of the morning when the coffee is cleared away and the last of the stragglers disappears out of the door. These candelabra are a sign of the symbol of the focus of the church; the people are bringing their best to God in worship, and only the best efforts are appropriate. And so they stay, lighting up the space between the altar and the heavens; Jesus the light of the world, acting as mediator for us, bridging the gap between where we are and where we want to be, lighting the way so that we can walk in it.

Most churches contain candles, the traditional symbol of Christ. Although the use of them might not be quite as free as the church I just mentioned, nearly all have two candles on the altar. In early times they had a practical use – to light the interior of the church, often in pitch darkness by Evensong. Then the church would be lit only by little pools of light at the altar and at the pulpit and lectern perhaps, illuminating the significant areas of the building. Even today some churches hold their carol services by candlelight. This can be stressful for the vergers perhaps, but these occasions are none the less wonderfully moving, celebrating as they do the birth of the saviour of the world with the sign of his love illuminating the darkness. The single small light of a candle can pierce our gloom and despair, reminding us that because of that first struggle in the darkness on the Mount of Olives, we are not alone; Jesus journeys with us, his light going before us to show the way.

Reflection

If you can, bring a candle with you into the church. It does not have to be a large one, but it needs to be able to stand alone. Find a seat in the middle of the body of the church – if you worship in this church, try not to sit in 'your' seat but in a different one. Light the candle and place it where you can see it without holding it. The candle gives out a very small amount of light; by daytime it hardly seems noticeable, at night it would do little to illuminate such a large building. And yet, day or night, it can clearly be seen, and our eyes are drawn to it. Once the entire church would have been lit by candles; now there is just this one. But there will be more – a few on Sunday perhaps, more at Christmas or Christingle. Candles are symbols of Christ, 'the light of the world'. This is a commonplace for us, but take some time to reflect on it. When things are going well for us, perhaps we are less aware of Christ's presence. It is only when the darkness threatens that the brightness of one single candle will shine out, stopping the darkness from overwhelming us.

Jesus, light of the world,
this candle reminds me how brief your life was on this earth.
Its light reminds me of the way you changed the world,

shining through the darkness of our wickedness.
Help me to see the light of your love in the dark times
so that I may not be overwhelmed.

This light is not just for us. We are given candles at our baptism
as a reminder not only that Christ is there for us but that we
in our turn must be there for others. Extinguish the candle and
think of someone who is in pain or suffering. Light the candle
again in his or her name and pray for that person.

Jesus, light of the world,
I pray for all who suffer, particularly for . . . .
Help them to be aware of your love for them,
bringing them comfort and healing in their pain.
Help me to shine as a light for them,
by my words and actions lighting the path to your love.

Starting point in the community – hospital/doctors' surgery

Our youngest son was not very well when he was born. Almost
immediately he was whisked away for a series of tests and other
procedures, leaving my husband and I rather adrift in a sea of
emotions, celebrations suspended as we did not have anyone to
celebrate with. We were allowed to take him home but the tests
continued. One afternoon we were driving to the city hospital for
a procedure that we had already been warned would be painful
and distressing. I turned to my husband who was driving, and
said, 'Where is Jesus now, in all this?' His eyes fixed firmly on the
road ahead my husband said, 'He's right here in the car with us,
of course.' And just for a moment I shared my husband's convic-
tion, and the worry and the fear lifted and I felt at peace. The

moment did not last long, and the anxiety soon flooded back in, but the memory of Presence supported me through the months ahead.

A doctor's surgery or a hospital waiting room is a powerful place to be. Filled with people whose stories we the observers may not even be able to imagine, there is at the same time a sense of the community of the sick and a feeling of desperate loneliness; very often an illness can isolate us in our fear and self-absorption, making us unable or unwilling to reach out for help. But, of course, these spaces are only gathering places for the struggling – temporary resting points where healing, or at least a lessening of the pain, is sought. The real struggle is in our daily lives when we try to continue our everyday occupations and tasks at the same time as trying to manage whatever struggle it is that we are engaged in.

It is in the struggle that prayer becomes our most powerful weapon, a reminder that whatever it may feel like, we are not alone, that Christ has been there before and that there is hope and redemption. It is where the prayers that we say when things are going well come into their own: a steady build-up of the fortifications of faith, a practising of our beliefs that can be a powerful resource to draw upon in those times when we feel unable to pray or when we have moved far from God.

We cannot avoid the struggle – it is part of our human existence – and the experiences that it brings can carry their own benefits and teaching. We can resolve to pray faithfully through them and to be sensitive to the pains of others. It is in these situations that being aware of community can be helpful. We can look to the community of the faithful of Old Testament times as we read some of the Psalms that echo our feelings both of abandonment and loss and of hope for the future and certainty in God. We can work within our church community to make the connections between individuals stronger and deeper, so that a change in behaviour in a fellow Christian is noticed and help and prayers offered. And we can join in with the prayers of the church for the suffering and the sick, bathing the struggle in the light of healing and love.

Reflection

Stand at the place where you have chosen to symbolize the struggling and pain that occurs in your community. Take out the stick you have with you and look at it. A stick can have very unhappy associations – it can remind us of the scourging of Christ just before he was taken away to be crucified. It reminds us of all those who are ill treated unjustly and cruelly. We can remember the injuries that are caused to people by others, and also the suffering that is nobody's fault, but simply a result of our human condition. The phrase 'you have made a rod for your own back' reminds us of the way that we ourselves are sometimes the cause of our own suffering.

> Lord, we pray for those who suffer
> in body, mind or spirit.
> For those for whom life has lost its joy
> and its meaning.
> We pray for those who live without hope
> or a knowledge of your love
> and we ask for your healing care
> to be poured out upon them.

A stick can also be used as a support. It is used to prop up growing things in the garden – fruit trees, young plants. Sticks are used by pilgrims to help them over the rough, difficult terrain that will form part of their journey, and to defend themselves from angry dogs which might attack them. So God's love can be a support for us, a prop in times of trouble and a help along the way.

God of strength and power
Help me to feel your support and guidance.
Help me to feel the might of your love,
holding me up when times are hard,
guiding me along the way.

5

The Heart of the Matter

Scripture reading
Luke 24.1–6 – 'He is not here; he has risen!'

Starting point at home
A table

Starting point in church
The altar

Starting point in the community
The focal point

What you will need
- *at home* – some bread
- *in church* – paper and crayons
- *in the community* – a bag for collecting litter and protective gloves if required

By about five o'clock that morning, I had given up even pretending that sleep was a possibility. The hostel I was in, though charming, was decidedly cramped, mostly due to the late arrival in the pouring rain of two more pilgrims than there were beds for. Those of us who had reached shelter before the downpour started did not have the heart to turn away the two soaking-wet Germans standing pathetically on the doorstep. As it happens, this was a bad decision for me, since they turned out to be champion snorers and, despite my tiredness, I could not find respite from their noise in sleep. Finally accepting that my night had ended, I dressed as quietly as possible, grabbed my backpack and, having refilled my water bottle, left the hostel.

It was still quite dark as I walked along, and as the path left the village and became simply a track once more, the noises of the night grew louder and more disquieting. Just when my limited stock of courage was beginning to run out, however, I noticed that even while I walked the sky had begun to lighten and the day had arrived.

When it got light enough to see what I was doing I stopped and lit my stove for a cup of tea. The track was running through open country by now, and from where I was sitting on the broad grass verge, I could see fields of lush green grass, dotted with large, placid cows. I could faintly hear dogs barking and cockerels waking up their farmsteads, but this was all in the distance. I felt in this brief moment a sense of connectedness with the whole of creation and with the One who created. This was what pilgrimage was all about, I thought, this the purpose of the journey, the tired legs, the lack of sleep, the continual slight anxiety at the edge of my consciousness – fear of running out of water, food or, worse still, the strength and will to continue. I took deep, satisfying breaths, content to be right in the moment, enjoying the now, the unity, the sheer wonder of it all.

The moment passed, as these moments must do, but the memory stayed and is with me still.

There are moments in our lives when things make sense, when it seems as if the answers to our questions will be revealed to us, or at least we become aware of the *possibility* of there being answers. At other times we might be overwhelmed by the apparent sheer pointlessness of our existence and the existence of others. In such moments, we as Christians must not give in to despair or allow ourselves to be destroyed by doubt. At the heart of our faith lies so great a love, such a deep compassion, that if we can but make our way there in trustful if faltering steps, there will be no need to question further, for he is the Answer.

Luke 24.1–6 – 'He is not here, he has risen!'

On the first day of the week, very early in the morning, the women took the spices they had prepared and went to the tomb. They found the stone rolled away from the tomb, but when they entered, they did not find the body of the Lord Jesus. While they were wondering about this, suddenly two men in clothes that gleamed like lightning stood beside them. In their fright the women bowed down with their faces to the ground, but the men said to them, 'Why do you look for the living among the dead? He is not here; he has risen!'

Some phrases can be extraordinarily powerful: 'I love you', 'I'm pregnant', 'He's gone', 'All clear'. Whole life stories can be summed up in just a few words: entire chains of events – hopes, anxieties, joys and surprises – can be guessed at, imagined, played out in our minds. And the phrase that appears in this Gospel reading is like these: 'He is not here; he has risen'. Seven words that sum up the Christian faith. Every time I read this story, I am captured again by the drama of the events. Imagine a grey dawn, the tomb in the half light, and the weary, saddened women making their way slowly towards it. They have come to perform the last tasks they possibly can for the one they loved so dearly, who held their hopes and their dreams in his hands. But now Jesus is dead and lies buried in the tomb, and their future, which had seemed so light, so large, is buried with him. What more can they do but seek to find acceptance of this in the rituals of caring for the dead? And then there comes the final blow – the tomb is empty. After all that has happened they have been robbed of their opportunity to say one last goodbye, to cherish that frail, broken body that they loved so much and that will now return to the dust from which it came. Who could have been so cruel? And then, in Luke's version, one of the two angels says the words that herald the start of a new life for the women and for all who believe: 'He is not here; he has risen'. Do not look for Jesus among the dead, you won't find him there. Do not seek to bury him beneath the bandages of ritual and procedure, beneath the dustiness of historical investigation or the dryness of scriptural exegesis. Do not look for Christ among those who say he was merely a good man or merely the perfect example for us to follow, for you will not find him there.

Jesus calls us 'children of the resurrection' (Luke 20.36). We must live like that – as if we believe what we say we believe, with all its implications for our lives: 'He is not here; he has risen'.

Starting point at home – a table

In the 20 years of our marriage we have lived in nine different houses. We have become very adept at moving, and at quickly finding the important places and necessary resources in our local community. The children have become so used to moving house and so energized by the whole concept of change, that at one time

I worried they would never experience the stability, the feeling of rootedness that comes from having lived in one place for a long time. Because of this worry, we established patterns and rituals for our lives that were transferable, that would be the same wherever we were, whatever house we lived in. The most significant of these focuses on the kitchen table – the same table, rather battered and with one very wobbly leg, that has been with us from the beginning. Hidden beneath a brightly coloured cloth, it bears the marks of toddlers banging their spoons in joyful anticipation of dinner, of forgetful teenagers putting hot dishes on its surface, of careless DIY 'experts' and their tools and paintbrushes. It has hosted birthday parties, Christmas lunches, anniversary dinners, business meetings and job interviews. And around this table every evening gathers whoever is in the house at the time, to share the time-honoured tradition of 'best bit of the day/worst bit of the day'. It is an opportunity to break news, to give vent to feelings of happiness or sadness, to voice joys and anxieties. We don't consciously pray together – differences of degrees of faith prevent that – but our sharing is like a prayer, reaffirming our commitment to one another, holding the family in community as they break bread together.

Simply because of its complete usefulness, and the utterly necessary nature of its function, there is a greater variety of type of table than of almost any other article of furniture. They share in common a flat surface, usually horizontal, but there the resemblance often ends. The difference between the massive refectory-style table, square and solid, that served medieval monasteries, and the fragile ornateness of the Georgian tea table could not be greater than between the ultra-high-fashion coloured-glass designer-labelled table found in chic city apartments and the chipped formica tabletop on four 'Utility' legs in my grandmother's kitchen. But it is at the table that people most often gather together, to share meals, drink tea or simply be in one another's company. It is at the kitchen table that the core of the home is found, where the hard work of preparing food, paying bills, writing letters – the actions that keep a home running – are all undertaken. It is at the table that Jesus showed us how to celebrate our life in community as Christians, remembering Christ's saving action for us and for the whole world. It is in breaking bread together that the first disciples retold the message of Christianity that would spread throughout the whole world: there is no need any longer to fear the tomb, the dark claustrophobia of death; 'He is not there; he has risen'.

Reflection

Find the table in your home that you consider the most significant for your life – it could be the kitchen table or one in a study or a dining room. Take time to look at it, to remember occasions when you have sat at it, to eat or to read, to meet people or to spend time alone. Remember the people who have sat at this table with you, meals you have eaten together or events you have shared.

Take a piece of bread in your hands. Bread in biblical times was more important than it is today in our era of varied diet, and preoccupation with calories and carbohydrates. The diners of Jesus' day did not use cutlery to eat, but would tear a piece of bread from a loaf to dip into a communal pot of food – one piece of bread for each mouthful of food. So bread was the means by which all food was received into the mouths of those at the table.

Jesus, bread of life,
I hold this bread in my hands and I thank you.
I have food to eat, and people to share this food with.
I pray for those who have neither.

Bread is the only material thing asked for in the Lord's Prayer – 'give us this day our daily bread'. So Jesus reminds us that we should ask only for that which is necessary to sustain us, but reassures us that this will be provided.

Jesus, bread of life,
So often I am concerned with the luxuries of life.
So often I seek comfort where I should seek truth.
So often I seek to please myself when I should care for others
    first.
Forgive me.

Our daily bread resonates with the time the children of Israel spent in the wilderness, when they stayed alive by eating manna, the bread from heaven, a direct gift of God. So too do we remember that we are daily dependent on God for his grace to sustain us.

Jesus, bread of life,
Help me to remember that I cannot live on this bread alone,
but that I am dependent on you.
Help me to make room in my self-preoccupation
for all that you would give me.

Break the bread, remembering Christ's sacrifice for us on the cross. Eat it slowly, celebrating the gift of life which this sacrifice brought to us.

Starting point in church – the altar

There are very few stone altars remaining in our Anglican parish churches, and those that do exist are often late replacements, after the furore of the Reformation had died. For it was declared that a stone altar brought with it too many connotations of human sacrifice, of frightened earthly bodies laid out for others to destroy with sharpened knives. The emphasis instead was to be on the community aspect – on the remembering and sharing in the company of others, a love so all-encompassing that it gladly took upon itself the burdens of others to the point of its own earthly destruction. So wooden tables were placed at the east end of the church building, usually covered with elaborate embroidered hangings and a white linen cloth laid on top.

The part of the building where the altar is found is usually differentiated from the rest. The altar itself may have a wooden rail which prevents the ordinary people encroaching too far on the holiest spaces. This in its turn may be set in an area that is accessed by a couple of steps, with the chancel, where the choir and church officials might sit, providing one more degree of distance from the congregation. Nowadays in some churches the congregation itself will sit in these pews ranged the length of the chancel, trying not to catch each other's eyes – although this is difficult if you are sitting opposite someone. The main service may well not place its focus at the high altar, fenced off as it is from the multitude, declaring its separateness, with only the priests being allowed into the sanctuary there to mediate between God and the people. The parish communion may be celebrated at another altar, placed in the middle of the nave, often at the crossing, where the nave meets the chancel and the side chapels stretch out their cruciform shape. Here the priest is among the people, speaking on their behalf, but with them as one of them, not a mediator but a fellow penitent, as unworthy as the rest of the community to share in the bread and wine but given the same gift of grace to enable them to approach confidently, without shame.

For it is at the altar that we must meet as equals in the sight of God, sharing between ourselves the love that he gives so freely, asking for nothing more than a return of that love, some small piece of that which was originally his. It is in the bread and the wine that we find the deepest mysteries of faith, so that as we eat and drink, however much we understand or believe, however great our fears or doubts, we are caught up in something beyond ourselves that makes us one.

Reflection

Bring a piece of paper and a pencil – or, better still, some crayons – with you into the church. Sit where you can see the altar and look at it quietly for a moment. Divide your paper into a pattern of square patches as if making a patchwork quilt. It can be a simple pattern, or something more geometrically complex, a few large blocks or several smaller ones. Into each square draw a picture of something that you wish to bring before God – it may be your home, for which you wish to give thanks, or the face of someone you know who is suffering, for whom you want to ask healing. You may want to draw the faces of those you love, or the faces of those you do not. You could draw an image that represents part of your life or a hobby you enjoy. Try to include some of the many different aspects of your life.

When you have drawn all you want to, place your altar 'cloth' upon the altar. Ask God, as you do this, to give you the grace to place your life into his hands.

Most Almighty God,
you hold in your hand

the earth and all that is in it.
Here is my life.
It is precious to you, I know.
Help me to be confident that I can rest in the shadow of your
  wings,
and that you will hold me safe.

Starting point in the community – the focal point

Perhaps nothing is as peculiar to a community as its focal point. This not only holds the heart of a community, often determining its direction and growth, if any, but can sum up the ethos of the neighbourhood. It does not have to be a place, this focal point; it could be an event or even a person. One of the reasons cited for the decline of a sense of community in rural settlements is the loss of the traditional 'lord of the manor' figure as so many of the large country estates have been forced by rising costs to sell up and relocate. These estates have either been broken up for sale in small lots or bought by those whose lives are not rooted in the community. One of the villages in which I worked was lucky enough still to have an inhabitant of the manor who believed strongly in her obligations to the village. Her gardens would host the village fete, her fields the bonfire party, and in winter the village sledges would congregate on the only good slope in the neighbourhood – the other side of her garden wall. She would willingly open her paddocks for use as a car park for big funerals, as well as sit on the various committees that are needed to keep a community functioning well. She was a regular church-goer and her amazing flower arrangements for festivals lifted the hearts of those who saw them. Truly at the heart of the village, she was a valuable part of its community.

In towns and cities, this immediate personal relationship may well not exist, but there may be groups or institutions that enable a community to thrive. The pub on the corner of the street where I live now has put much effort into becoming a part of the local life of the area – it hosts reading groups, organizes mums' coffee mornings, puts on special events, and makes a room available for the numerous small committees and groups who need somewhere to meet that is bigger than a private house but smaller than a hall. All this takes its toll on the property, time and energy of the focal point and it is this that so often deters people from contributing as much as they could. For the most part unrecognized and unthanked, many people are discouraged by the difficulties of helping a community to flourish, but it is only through sacrificial giving that this growth can occur, especially if the community is a disjointed or disheartened one.

As Christians we believe that we can only flourish as part of a community. We must take our part in encouraging neighbourhoods to share the resources of the areas in which they live in a mutually beneficial way, even if the cost to us is initially quite high. Joining local groups, attending meetings of local action committees or, if this is beyond us, reading the local newspaper and praying for the items that impact on our local environment, all are the actions of people who know that they cannot travel alone but must do so in the company of others.

Reflection

Find the place that for you is the heart of your community. It may be the church, the pub or the community centre. It could be the home of an individual, or the place where a local action group meets. Stand outside it and ask God's blessing on it.

Starting from this place, walk on, collecting any litter or rubbish that you find, praying as you go so that in one small way the neighbourhood might be improved by your presence.

Lord, I see on the streets
evidence of neglect,
of people who are too busy,
or who don't care enough.
I am sorry for those actions which damage community
and for my part in them.
As I pick up these bits of litter,
making the streets a better place to be,
help me in my words and actions
to enable this community to grow and flourish,
reflecting your love.

6

Resting

Scripture reading
Luke 24.49 – Wait!

Starting point at home
Chair or bed

Starting point in church
The nave

Starting point in the community
Places of leisure

What you will need
- *at home* – objects to make a place for prayer: a candle, perhaps some flowers, an icon
- *in church* – nothing!
- *in the community* – a watch, a mobile, or something that tells the time

We all find our places and methods of rest and recreation in different ways. That is one of the wonderful things about human beings. We need only remember first that our way of relaxing is not the only way. Just because the idea of sitting for long hours on a river bank trying to catch fish that will only be thrown back again, or walking round houses and gardens that were once owned by the rich, holds no appeal for us does not mean that these things have no value. As long as our methods of rest and recreation are not harmful to ourselves, others or the environment, every way is a good way. The most important thing of all is to ensure that we do indeed make time for things other than the daily round of work and household chores.

Luke 24.49 – Wait!

> I am going to send you what my Father has promised; but stay in the city until you have been clothed with power from on high.

This is Jesus' last instruction to the disciples before he ascends into heaven and leaves them to spread the message to all of his saving action. And what an interesting instruction it is. Jesus does not say to the disciples: 'rush out immediately and tell everyone the good news of my resurrection'. He does not tell them to go about doing good deeds – healing the sick, giving money to the poor. He does not even tell them to get themselves organized for what will surely be a long and difficult campaign, to tidy things up, sort out their admin, write a few leaflets or design a poster or two. No, Jesus tells his disciples simply to stay in the city and wait. They have very important things to do in the future, and their lives will not be easy ones. They will be travelling, sometimes escaping and hiding from those who would silence them.

They will preach, teach and heal. They will found churches and help to run them. They will face angry crowds, hostile judges. They will be imprisoned and beaten, and some of them will die. But for now there is the command to wait, to rest, to gather their strength. They need to reflect on the wonderful events of the recent past, so much in contrast with the terror and despair of the crucifixion and the nightmare of a trial that led up to it. They need to remember Jesus' teaching, his love, his readiness to seek out the poor and the outcast, his scorn for the way things are and this announcement of the way things will be. All this can only be assimilated in a period of calm and of apparent inaction. The time for action will soon be upon them. The time for rest is now.

So too must we make sure that our actions are preceded and followed by times of rest. Following the rhythms of the earth, the rhythms God gave us, we have arrived once more in a time of quiet and relaxation. Let us wait together.

Starting point at home – chair or bed

The chair is so much a part of our everyday life that we scarcely give it a moment's thought. Certainly in its rudimentary form of an object designed to raise the sitter from the floor, it has existed almost as long as human beings have. Crouching round a fire in a cave, the urge to use the piece of wood that is next to the fire to lift oneself off the cold ground must have been instinctive and unthinking. There is evidence of stools, benches and chairs in ancient Egyptian and Chinese drawings and paintings, although, interestingly, the use of a chair with a back and arms as opposed to a stool with neither was confined for thousands of years to the nobility and the ruling classes. It is from this, it is believed, that the expression is derived of 'chair' for the leader of a group or meeting. This person would literally have been the only person to sit in a chair. With the Renaissance, however, chairs became more plentiful and fairly soon they were used by everyone. It is in these times that the almost infinite variety of style and design of chair began to develop. Chairs, while remaining as objects with a practical function, became highly decorative and ornamental as well, subject like other smaller items of furniture to the changing moods of fashion. They reflected Georgian delicacy, Victorian solidarity, postwar minimalism: echoing the mood of the age, following the feeling of the times.

Today almost any type and style of chair can be found in our homes, from the basic 'four legs, one seat, one back' stackable affair in light plastic, through the more rugged wooden chair that is placed at so many kitchen and dining tables, up to the comfortable expansiveness of the fully upholstered armchair into which one can sink at the end of the day. This sort of chair can become a focal point for personal rest and relaxation and it is quite easy to get possessive about it. When visiting people in their homes very often I would be invited into the living room. I had a few seconds, half a minute at the most, to look around and decide on which chair to sit. There were two types I always avoided. The chair the dog sat on was the most obvious one – if I sat on this one, I invariably stood up covered in dog hairs. However, I also tried to avoid sitting in the homeowner's chair – to sit in this would make him or her unsettled and feel a bit put out, often subconsciously, thus making the visit more difficult. The owner's chair was usually easy to spot – it was most likely the largest, often nearest the fire, with the best view of the television. There would be a table to one side, sometimes one each side, on which would be all the things necessary for leisure time – the day's paper, a book or magazine perhaps, space for a drink and, of course, the television remote!

It is interesting how often we associate our moments of leisure and rest with a particular piece of furniture, usually the chair, although occasionally we might feel we are not fully relaxed until we finally make it into bed. This association becomes a spiral – if we sit in the chair to relax regularly we find that we sit in the chair in order to relax, and so on. This spiral can also be used in a different way, adding to and enhancing our moments of rest. For those of us who feel that our prayer life is often erratic and rather unsatisfactory, it is possible to add on to our sitting-down ritual a brief moment to pause and pray. If this is consistently carried out – for example, if we say a brief prayer as soon as we sit down – it becomes a habit. Our chairs become associated with prayer and rest, a habit that can be extended if we wish, so that a daily prayer time becomes as much a part of our routine as reading the paper or watching the news. Just as the disciples were told to stay in the city until given the power of the Spirit, sometimes it is in the waiting, the pause, the reflection, that those moments of insight – gifts of the Spirit – can be given.

Reflection

Walk round the place where you live, trying to discern what would be your place of relaxation within it. It may be a living-room armchair: where you sit at the end of the day. It may be a chair at the kitchen table where you pause for coffee in the morning, or your moments of rest may have to wait until you retire for the night. Once you have identified it, spend some time trying to make it a place of prayer as well. You may want to put a candle on a table next to it, with a box of matches to ensure that you don't have to jump up again as soon as you have sat down. You may also want to put a small icon, some flowers or something else you find beautiful, on the table as well – anything that marks the place as special. Make sure that any prayer materials are near at hand – if you use a specific book, for example, but usually keep it in a different place, it may be worth buying an extra copy just for this chair. Once this space is prepared it is a simple matter of committing yourself to pause briefly every time you sit there, resting in God for a moment before moving on to your leisure activity. If practised regularly you will find that this becomes unconscious, your mind being habituated to prayer and all that it offers.

God of time and space, God of eternity,
this is my favourite place in the house.
It is where I sit when I relax,
it is where my time belongs to me.
Help me to share this time with you,
Creator of all, giver of time itself.

Starting point in church – the nave

The nave of the church is where the body of the people sit – those people who faithfully, or not so faithfully, attend the weekly services of the church as frequently as they are willing or able. It is this part of the church that most often reflects the various stages of growth and development that took place in the life of the building. In some places you can see how the gentle curves of a Roman arch sharpen into the pointed ones of the Gothic period, influenced as much by an increasing skill and ability on the part of stonemasons and carpenters as by the changing styles of architectural fashion. Here too can often be seen the side chapels built in honour of donors to the church, so that later generations may pray for their souls.

The nave will also contain many clues as to the preferences of the congregation worshipping in the church today. Maybe they cling steadfastly to the rows of pews introduced after the Middle Ages, when the use of the building for anything other than worship was frowned upon, and there was no need to keep the main area clear of the markets and other activities of former times. Or perhaps these rows of rather uncomfortable seating have been swept away, auctioned off to raise funds for the more comfortable chairs now in their place. There may be a hymn board showing the number of last Sunday's hymns, or the equipment for a projector and a large screen so that the congregation do not have to hold their own books but can look forward and up, together. Evidence of any work with children will be seen in the nave – a children's corner perhaps, or even a glassed-off area. Display boards and posters may show the different children's groups and activities. Here too among the notices will be found the clues to the congregation's interests – a myriad posters advertising musical concerts or campaign meetings, theological lectures, or mothers' fellowship groups. All these point to the nature of the community and its relationship with the outside world.

So why, therefore, in the midst of this bustle and activity, given a rhythm by the weekly services of the church, is the nave, this large expanse of space, the place for rest and recreation? It might be thought that the intimacy of a side chapel would be more appropriate, or the privacy of a vestry. I think the answer lies in its very everydayness – after all, it is in the midst of the ordinary things of life that the great, the painful, the difficult are present. I have worked for many years for the church and spent many hours in church buildings – it is where I write my books and often my sermons as well. Very rarely, during the periods I am in church, do I spend that entire time by myself. Even if the church is one of those forlorn creatures that is kept locked, it is surprising just how many people own a key to the building.

Many times when I am praying or thinking or writing, people will wander in, sometimes looking round the building for a few minutes before they sit down. And they sit in the nave. It is the place that holds best our thoughts and our prayers, the place with which we are most familiar if we are members of the congregation, and seems the least intrusive if we are not. It is in the nave Sunday by Sunday that we offer our struggles and our pain to God, praying for healing for ourselves and others, asking for help through difficult times, companionship in lonely hours. It is in the nave that the solitary visitor will sit, in the hope of finding peace and comfort.

I remember one winter afternoon when, wearing as many clothes as possible, I was finishing a sermon in a small village church. A man entered. He noticed me, nodded briefly, sat down and began to cry – loud, painful sobs of someone not used to emotions. He cried for about half an hour, his head in his hands. When he had more or less stopped I went over to him and put my hand on his shoulder. 'I'm fine,' he said. 'It is the anniversary of my wife's death. I have nowhere else to go to cry because I have to be strong for the children. I don't go to church, but thank you for the use of your building.'

We look pain straight in the eyes in the nave of the church, but we can find comfort and rest there too. In the reading, the disciples are given time to reflect on their experiences so far, to incorporate them into their being, to absorb the knowledge that they have gained and to begin to act on it and live in it. Taking time out of our daily occupations and actions can allow the knowledge and experience we receive to affect our way of living. By reflecting on our actions and learning from this reflection, allowing it to change and develop further actions, we can grow in our understanding of ourselves and of God.

Reflection

This is one of the simplest and perhaps the most difficult of all reflections. Simply choose a place in the nave to sit, make yourself comfortable, and be still. Take time to look around the church, to stare perhaps at the things that you have not given much time to before, noticing small details that have escaped your attention. Think about the people who made these things. Allow your mind to wander – just for these few minutes it does not matter what you think about; just enjoy the act of sitting and resting.

Lord God, you created the world in six days
and blessed the seventh by resting.
Help me to balance my life with action and inaction,
work and rest.
Give me the gift of resting in you,
allowing your hands to hold me and all my concerns,
feeling surrounded by your love,
safe and at peace.

Starting point in the community – places of leisure

It is early in the morning and the park is the preserve of the joggers and keep-fit enthusiasts. Many simply run through it – their aims are further afield, their target of miles more ambitious than a few circuits of what is after all only a medium-sized field. Others doggedly run five or six times around the outside of the park along the canal towpath that forms one of its borders, stopping at the benches for various stretching and strengthening exercises before heading home via the local paper shop.

Then it is the turn of the schoolchildren taking extravagant diversions on their bikes or scooters or simply running in wild zigzags from path to goal posts, practising tricks and jumps, shadowing less fortunate friends firmly attached to pushchairs or gripped by parents' hands, preventing them from straying off route. These are the same parents who after the school drop-off will pause in the children's play area to allow toddlers the opportunity to explore their environment without the often tyrannical accompaniment of older siblings. The mothers sit and chat, eyes constantly swivelling, interspersing conversation with shouts of admonishment and encouragement. Then children are gathered up as parents head home to housework or toddler group, leaving the park to the dog walkers who emerge once the noise and tumult of young children has died down. The dogs run and chase one another, the owners occasionally exchanging a few words, or reassuring nervous walkers slightly overwhelmed by the number of leash-free canines.

As the sun warms the benches the readers emerge: flat-dwellers or perhaps those who need some vitamin D to keep them going for the rest of the day. They walk singlemindedly to their favourite bench, the one that offers the right degree of sunshine and shade, then sink into their books, motionless for minutes or hours depending on their timetable. Some are only chased away by the arrival of the pre-school pick-up troupe, those mums and toddlers waiting for their siblings. Any hardy readers who determinedly cling to their benches are soon edged off them by the non-stop chatter and activity of small children and their carers.

The activity level increases; school has ended and children fill the green space, running, playing football, plunging into the narrow strip of woodland that edges one side of the park. The action continues more or less unabated until the arrival of the older children from secondary school, who take over the football goal, easing the smaller children out simply by kicking harder, faster and more often. They settle on the benches, swinging their legs, eating crisps, smoking and chatting. They mean no harm, but mothers anxiously gather up the younger ones who have been watching open-mouthed, savouring the rich, unfamiliar words and expressions, envying their careless freedoms. This group holds sway for the evening hours, eyed warily by the after-work joggers, who do not linger for fear of overhearing unfavourable remarks on their speed and fitness shouted after them with scornful laughter. Even these are eventually driven in by the dark, the cold and hunger pangs, until there is only one lone basketball player, shooting hoops as he waits for his girlfriend to finish her shift in the local shop.

At last the park is still, silent in the few brief hours of the night before the dawn brings the start of the cycle again.

The areas in our community that are dedicated to rest and relaxation are a vital and precious part of our neighbourhood. They hold the area's laughter, its fun, its ability to recover from the demands that are made upon it. We should be proud of the amenities our area has to offer, whether they are theatres, cinemas, leisure-centre parks or simply patches of greenery where people can pause for a while. As part of our task as intercessors for each community, we need to recognize the value of all these places and join in the efforts to preserve and improve them because they are one of the many threads that bind our neighbourhood together.

Reflection

First, make a sort of mental inventory of the places of recreation in your neighbourhood. These may be cinemas, leisure centres, theatres, the village hall or the local pubs. There may be green spaces – parks or public gardens or woodland. If you wish, you could collect leaflets from each one and make them into a collage, perhaps putting them on a notice board near the place where you pray or somewhere you will see them frequently. Then regularly choose a place to pray for. Walk to that place, spend some time observing it and praying for the people who work there and visit it.

Take out your watch or something that tells the time. Stand still for a moment, observing how time moves on so quickly.

Imagine your life is a 24-hour clock – how far through has the clock ticked? Are you at the beginning, at about 4 a.m., when the future is all before you and nothing is yet planned? Are you in the middle, at noon, leading a busy life full of commitments and obligations? Are you nearing the end of your time on earth?

Consider what you will do with the time you have left upon this earth. Ask God to help you spend your time wisely, balancing work and leisure, the demands of others and your need for space. Pray that you may always have the grace to make time for God.

God of green fields and still waters,
God of theatres and swimming pools,
God of football stadiums and racetracks,
God of dolls' houses and woodwork,
God of rest, of silent absorption and of noisy laughter:
Bless our places of leisure and entertainment.
Help us to find what we need in them.
Help us to respect the pastimes of others,
and to see your hand in all.

7

Remembering

Scripture reading
Luke 24.13–35 – the road to Emmaus

Starting point at home
Photographs

Starting point in church
Memorials

Starting point in the community
Places of memory

What you will need
- *at home* – a family photograph
- *in church* – paper and pen
- *in the community* – a British Legion poppy or a fresh flower

Memory is a powerful thing. I have sat by the bedside of very old people as they lie, often in pain, holding their hands and listening to their stories. I have marvelled that these stories are still so vivid and so immediate that they have brought tears not only to the eyes of the person telling the story, but to the listener as well. I have leaned low over the dying, just catching the words of the Lord's Prayer that we say together – all other words forgotten, just those that have become so deeply etched on the heart and soul and mind of the faithful that their imprint survives all traumas. Even when minds themselves fade and muddle, a few stories, mental images, or recollections will remain, as clear and as focused as the day the events were experienced.

Our memories can be painful and disturbing – sometimes events have happened that are so dreadful and traumatic that they are buried deep in the subconscious, occasionally reappearing, to our horror, triggered by some word, some action of another person or some place that reminds us of the past and brings it back to life, fresh and raw as ever. Other memories can keep us going through difficult times, giving us confidence that these moments will pass and enabling us to hope for a better future.

All these memories, even the bad ones, have value in our lives. They are part of what shaped us and make us who we are today. We must recognize this and ask God to transform our bad memories and reinforce our good ones so that our words and actions may be clear pathways for his love.

Luke 24.13–35 – the road to Emmaus

Now that same day two of them were going to a village called Emmaus, about seven miles from Jerusalem. They were talking with each other about everything that had happened. As they talked and discussed these things with each other, Jesus himself came up and walked along with them; but they were kept from recognising him.

He asked them, 'What are you discussing together as you walk along?'

They stood still, their faces downcast. One of them, named Cleopas, asked him, 'Are you only a visitor to Jerusalem and do not know the things that have happened there in these days?'

'What things?' he asked.

'About Jesus of Nazareth,' they replied. 'He was a prophet, powerful in word and deed before God and all the people. The chief priests and our rulers handed him over to be sentenced to death, and they crucified him; but we had hoped that he was the one who was going to redeem Israel. And what is more, it is the third day since all this took place. In addition, some of our women amazed us. They went to the tomb early this morning but didn't find his body. They came and told us that they had seen a vision of angels, who said he was alive. Then some of our companions went to the tomb and found it just as the women had said, but him they did not see.'

He said to them, 'How foolish you are, and how slow of heart to believe all that the prophets have spoken! Did not the Christ have to suffer these things and then enter his glory?' And beginning with Moses and all the Prophets, he explained to them what was said in all the Scriptures concerning himself.

As they approached the village to which they were going, Jesus acted as if he were going further. But they urged him strongly, 'Stay with us, for it is nearly evening; the day is almost over.' So he went in to stay with them.

When he was at the table with them, he took bread, gave thanks, broke it and began to give it to them. Then their eyes were opened and they recognised him, and he disappeared from their sight. They asked each other, 'Were not our hearts burning within us while he talked with us on the road and opened the Scriptures to us?'

They got up and returned at once to Jerusalem. There they found the Eleven and those with them, assembled together and saying, 'It is true! The Lord has risen and has appeared to Simon.' Then the two told what had happened on the way, and how Jesus was recognised by them when he broke the bread.

The story of the events that happened to those dispirited disciples on the road to Emmaus is one of the most beautiful in the world. It tells of a transformation from the darkness of despair to the light of a love-filled hope and a new outlook upon the world. It is short, simple and utterly powerful and contains some lyrical insights into the nature of Christian healing.

The road to Emmaus lies to the west of Jerusalem. The disciples were heading towards the sunset. Perhaps it was because the light of the setting sun was in their eyes and dazzled them that they did not recognize him. Perhaps it was because they were looking in the wrong place for him. For the disciples it was already over – Jesus had died and, with him, all their hopes for a new and different future. Gone were those times of loving companionship, of learning to see the world in a different way, of witnessing the amazing power of Jesus' healing miracles. Instead there was only the fading light of another ending day.

As Christians we should not be looking towards the sunset but towards the east, expectant of a new dawn, a new beginning, a new world; if we allow hope and anticipation to fade and die, then all that is vital within us will gradually fade.

So tumultuous are the feelings of the disciples, so fresh the emotions of betrayal and loss that came upon them at the death of their master, that their reaction to this stranger's enquiry as to the subject of their conversation is one of incredulity. They are almost rude in their relation of events – surely no one could be unaware of the disaster that had overtaken the hopes of Israel, trustingly placed in the fragile human being who had been broken so cruelly on the cross. But patiently and carefully Jesus talks to them, encourages them to a new understanding. So too do we often need to take time to gain understanding of the events that have happened to us. Sometimes we need others to help us to understand; sometimes our dependence on strangers is a necessary part of the healing process.

When they arrive at their lodgings, Jesus at first makes as if to move on, but the disciples urge him to stay with them and talk further. Jesus offers his love, his companionship, his healing freely, but not forcefully. It is up to us to decide whether to invite him into our lives – he knocks, but we are the ones who must open the door. Healing of any kind cannot occur until we ask for it in trust and love, accepting the fact that we may not understand the reason for everything at once, that events may not happen as we wish according to the schedule we think we need, recognizing that allowing Jesus into our lives is the first crucial step to wholeness.

And so Jesus sits with them and breaks bread and it is in this breaking of the bread that enlightenment occurs and the disciples recognize him for who he is. Perhaps they remember the last time he broke bread with them; perhaps he places the miracles of the transforming action right into the heart of the most ordinary events. It is in the faithful enactment of the everyday that we will see God.

Starting point at home – photographs

One of the first things we often notice when we enter somebody's home is the photographs. Some houses have very few pictures, just a faded wedding photograph on a side table, or a snapshot of a grandchild recently arrived and proudly displayed on the mantelpiece. Others have tables and cupboards whose surfaces bristle with frames, and walls whose original colour can hardly be seen for the many faces staring out of the assorted collection of frames hanging there.

Photographs occupy a strange, liminal place in our home. They are intensely personal things, records of moments that are usually of no significance except to those in the picture and the person who displays it. They capture moments of academic or public achievement; they record the stages of a family's growth and development – wedding portraits often alongside those of a christening group, perhaps nudging up against those touching formal school portraits that give an air of awkwardness to the most captivating child. There are holiday snaps and party times, all triggering memories and recollections – if not of the event itself then at least of the people shown at it. The curious onlooker has no such emotional connections; they see merely an assorted collection of people, much like any other group. It is interesting to take a closer look and remark on family resemblance, perhaps, or the fleeting nature of fashion that renders older pictures faintly comic. And yet the observer would do well not to peer too closely for fear of being thought overly inquisitive, rudely poking one's nose into private family matters. For although those photographs are on public display they are not really for public gaze. For the most part we are wise to let our eyes roam only briefly over the assorted collection, unless invited to look more closely at a particular portrait proffered for our inspection.

Although we do not believe that the taking of a photograph captures part of the subject's soul, perhaps it is possible to see into his or her soul if we look closely . . .

Reflection

Photographs are a way of reminding ourselves of the friends and family to whom we are connected, even if they are not physically present. They can help remind us, when things are not going so well for us, of the good times, giving us confidence that the good times will in due course happen again. They can encourage us to remember that we are not alone and to rejoice in the affection we have both given and received.

Photographs can be a way of making intercessions more immediate. Try looking at the photographs you have on display, pausing to pray briefly for each person or group that is shown, thanking God for their lives, asking his blessing on their futures.

You could make an intercessions album, collecting together perhaps one picture of each member of your family or close friends as a reminder to you to pray for that person. If this album is of the scrapbook variety, prayer requests can also be written down on a particular page. It is important to write down the date of these requests so that later you might be able to write down a date when they were answered, or at least a solution arrived at. In this way your intercession book can become a wonderful record of God's action in your life and in the lives of others. I know of one family who has just such an intercessions album. The members of the family pictured in the book are encouraged to write any prayer requests they have on the page with their photograph on it, so that their mother can pray with more direction when she comes to look on their page. This encourages the children to feel involved in the act of prayer, and to witness for themselves the answers to their prayers.

Starting point in church – memorials

Church memorials are a curious thing. There are some churches that are literally covered in small brass plaques, almost every object being donated in memory of a tireless worker for the church or of a much-loved and missed partner or child. The doors, the pews, the silver, even the linen, may be marked with a carefully worded dedication. They are a way, perhaps, for those who mourn to keep some contact with the person they loved – every week the object reminds that person of the nature and character of their companion, friend, lover, child. They remind us that we are not the first people to worship in the building. Generations of men, women and children have polished the brass, swept the floor, worried about the linen and raised funds for the roof, caring for the interior and exterior of the building with a love and pride that have kept the building alive and functioning. They are also a reminder to us that we too have a part to play in supporting the church in a physical way if we are to ensure its continuation for the following generations.

But the church is not solely about buildings; the church is not primarily an arrangement of stone or bricks, decorated inside with wood, silver and brass. The purpose of the church building is to house the church – that community of people who gather week by week in faith, trying to live out the gospel commands of Christ as well as they can, learning slowly and painfully how best to love God and their neighbours.

I have seen many wonderful and awe-inspiring monuments. I have gazed at huge stained-glass windows, which refract and reflect the light into a multitude of colours, dancing on the stone floor, joyfully echoing the scene of the window above. I have seen beautifully carved statues of saints and bishops, their smooth surfaces showing the skill of the sculptor. I have marvelled at the intricacies of the tombs that commemorate their inhabitants, with their complicated symbolism and stylized faces. But all these fade beside the most beautiful monument I have ever seen. It is in a church where I worshipped when I was first married. It is in memory of the vicar of that village who served his parish long and faithfully. He was an intelligent man; his sermons were always interesting, although his administration was rather on the sketchy side and his study looked as if a paper monster had run riot in it. But these are just insignificant details. This man loved God, and this love shone through him to his parishioners. More importantly even than this, however, was the fact that his parishioners could *see* God shining through him. This vicar, by his words and behaviour, acted as a window, through which those who wished to could see God. There was something about his character, his nature, his way of loving, that made him transparent to God. And I was not alone in recognizing this quality. When he died, it was decided that if anyone deserved a memorial in the church he had served so faithfully and well, it was him. But his parishioners wanted a memorial that reflected his nature. Therefore it was decided that instead of commissioning a chair or a piece of silver, they would remove the opaque glass from one of the windows in a side chapel and replace it with clear glass. The congregation can now sit bathed in light in the church and gaze out on to the trees and the sky, evidence of God's love in creation.

Jesus' appearance to those poor, dispirited disciples, his conversation and his company, reminded them of what it was like to walk alongside him. The disciples shared their joy in all they had learnt from him, eager to make this stranger understand how it felt to be a disciple. And they continued to learn, as Jesus, still unrecognized, explained all that was written by the prophets concerning him. We too can commit ourselves to continual learning and also to sharing our own experiences and wisdom with others. For it is in this community of learning, of sharing, of gathering together, that Christ will be recognized as being among us – just as it is in the communal meal at the end of the day that the disciples finally see Jesus 'in the breaking of the bread'.

Reflection

Spend a few moments walking round your church looking at the memorials. Some older ones may be in Latin, but many, particularly those of more recent years, will be easy to read. Take special note of the things that were thought to be important to be known about the person to whom the object is dedicated. Then take some time to think about how you would like to be remembered. What sort of object would you most like to be given to the church in your memory: a silver candlestick to indicate the light that Christ has been in your life, perhaps; or would you rather be remembered with something more practical, such as refurbishment of the doors, or something relevant to your interests – maybe books for the Sunday School?

Once you have decided on an object, spend some time thinking what you would like written on this object. Limit yourself to 25 words. How do you think you will be remembered? How would you *like* to be remembered? Are these two things different? If so, how could you change the way you live, the things you do and say, so that you will be remembered as you would most prefer?

God of the living and the dead,
help me to live rightly
so that when I die
I will be remembered
not for myself alone
but for the work you did through me.

Starting point in the community – places of memory

One of the interesting things for me about this project has been trying to discern which are the features of a village or town or city that are held in common by almost every community of whatever size. I have included churches, places of healing, places of rest and recreation, aiming to be as general and inclusive as possible. It is a sad fact of our nation's history that one of the more specific things that almost every community has is a memorial to those soldiers who died in the two great wars of the twentieth century. Even the smallest settlement has its commemorative plaque, cross or monument, with the names of those who died engraved upon it. In fact, the smaller the settlement the more poignant this memorial can be, as the five or six families whose names listed upon it are likely still to be represented in the list of current inhabitants; and the disproportionately large part of the population that was taken away in those wars makes more vivid the scale of the destruction. In one tiny village that was part of my 'patch' at one time, three families had between them lost seven sons, and this loss had decimated the population of that community.

During my time as a priest I have had the privilege of listening to people's memories of their lives and the lives of those they loved. I have heard a few wartime anecdotes. People talked about the officers they had known and what they had thought of them, about the food that they had to eat, and how it was different from what the Americans had. They talked about the practical joke that had been pulled on someone. Aside from these things, often little is said about the actual war. What they really remembered best, they did not speak of.

This can be the case with other parts of our lives as well – particularly those bits that were painful or unhappy. It can be hard to talk about the details of something that happened, the real cost of our choices or the pain caused to us by others, how our own minds and hearts were affected by events and never again quite the same. In the case of war memorials, an entire community's memories and identity for one part of its history are on display, which in turn can affect the present and the future. For ourselves and our own lives, our memories and how we deal with them can affect our attitude to our own future and to our relationship with others. For some of us, healing will be found in sharing these memories; for others it is in letting them go. For all of us, we have a duty to acknowledge the pain of others – that which is privately hidden as well as that which is publicly recognized. We can do this by living responsibly and gratefully, giving thanks for those who spent their lives working for others, sometimes losing their lives in the process. We can commit ourselves to living in such a way that we do not break faith with those who died to bring peace to the world. We can accept responsibility for our actions on a small scale within the community, and on a large scale by recognizing that we play a part in deciding the actions of our country within the world arena.

And finally, we can rejoice in other memorials that are erected in thanksgiving, in gratitude, in celebration. We can pause by the blue plaques that commemorate the dwelling place of those who contributed to the life of the nation – writers, artists, scientists. We can marvel at buildings that mark national events such as those dedicated to Silver Jubilees or the Millennium. And we can stop by the humble park bench and pray for the person whose name is inscribed on a small brass plate on the backrest, whose humble contribution to the world may be forgotten by many but whose life was clearly cherished.

Reflection

The traditional way of honouring those people who have died in public service is that of laying individual poppies or wreaths of poppies at a war memorial. If it is at all near Remembrance Sunday these will be easy to obtain; if this proves more challenging, for this reflection any flower will be appropriate. Simply take a flower and lay it at the site of your local memorial. If you can, say the Act of Remembrance, and remain silent for a minute or two.

ACT OF REMEMBRANCE

Let me remember before God, and commend to his sure
    keeping:
those who have died for their country in war;
those whom I knew, and whose memory I treasure;
and all who have lived and died in the service of mankind.

They shall grow not old as we that are left grow old:
Age shall not weary them, nor the years condemn.
At the going down of the sun and in the morning
I will remember them.

Silence

Ever-living God, I remember those whom you have gathered
from the storm of war into the peace of your presence;
may that same peace calm our fears, bring justice to all peoples
and establish harmony among the nations, through Jesus Christ
our Lord. Amen.

Lord's Prayer

RESPONDING IN HOPE AND COMMITMENT

The Kohima Epitaph
When you go home, tell them of us and say,
for your tomorrow we gave our today.

May the souls of the faithful departed rest in peace.
And rise in glory.

I commit myself to responsible living and faithful service.
I will strive for all that makes for peace.
I will seek to heal the wounds of war.
I will work for a just future for all humanity.
God, I offer to you the fears in me
that have not yet been cast out by love:
May I accept the hope you have placed in the hearts of all
    people,
and live a life of justice, courage and mercy; through Jesus
    Christ
our risen Redeemer. Amen.

8

Beginning Again

Luke 24.52–53

Then they worshipped him and returned to Jerusalem with great joy. And they stayed continually at the temple, praising God.

And so Luke's Gospel ends where it began, in the temple, praising God, the beginning and end of all that is meaningful in our lives. What started with an old man, bravely managing the sadness of his childless state, finishes with a group of joyful people whose lives have been transformed.

And our pilgrimages end where they began, returning to the front door, the font, the boundary of the community. Back where we started, we can collect our thoughts, put back the things we used for reflections. We have taken time away from our everyday preoccupations, our normal habits, and sought God. And if we have sought him diligently, we will find him, often where we least expect to, right in the middle of our ordinary lives, filling our daily occupations with his love and his light until they are transformed.

Just as precious diamonds are dull and rough when they are first hewn out of the rock, so our lives can seem as if they carry no meaning, reflect no light. It is only through careful attention to detail, the accurate cutting and polishing of each tiny surface of the stone, that the full glory of the diamond can shine through, multi-coloured light sparkling out of every facet, shot through with rainbows. So it is only with careful journeying – mindful, prayerful walking, pausing at each place on our journey – that we can catch a glimpse of the sacred nature within, that transfuses our everyday and makes every place holy ground.

9

Waymarks and Cairns

It was Boxing Day and after two days of hard work and good food, we were desperate for fresh air. Accordingly we all piled into the car and set off for our favourite walk in the Brecon Beacons. The weather, not good at the start of the journey, became gradually worse, until by the time we got to the bottom of our chosen peak, visibility was rather poor. We put on all our rough-weather gear, which included taking a rope with us, since we always plan for the worst. As we walked up the hill it started to snow harder until it was very difficult to see. Only the fact that the path was well trodden and very familiar to us made the walk at all possible.

The peak of this particular mountain is very large and flat – it is less a peak than a plateau, in fact – and it is here that route-finding, always challenging, became truly taxing in the poor weather conditions. My husband, a champion navigator, kept his eyes glued to his compass, pausing frequently to check readings against the map, much to our consternation, as we often did not notice that he had stopped until we bumped into him. However, even he was getting apprehensive – if we did not locate the peak properly, we stood no chance of finding the direct, easier and therefore safer route down the mountain. It was with a huge feeling of relief therefore that out of the swirling white of snow there suddenly loomed the large, solid heap of stones that was the cairn marking the summit. Crouching in the lee of the cairn, sheltered from the wind, we rapidly consumed some bars of chocolate and I took a swig of tea from my thermos, before heading down the mountain again, reassured that we were walking in the right direction.

As we walked quickly downhill, I reflected on the vital – even life-saving – role that the cairn had played, not just for us but for many hundreds of walkers before us. Without that stern grey monument, many hours might be spent wandering around on the plateau at the summit, draining energy levels and using precious daylight hours looking for the safest way down.

There is a similar cairn halfway along the route to Santiago de Compostela, but its purpose is different. Route-finding is not a particularly challenging issue on this walk – by the time you have arrived at this particular heap of stones, the route has been trodden bare by the tens of thousands of pilgrims who walk the way of St James each year. Nor, however, is it merely a straightforward sign that the halfway route has been reached – it has a deeper significance than that. For this cairn is not made up of a few large stones skilfully balanced on top of one another by stonesmen so that they remain in place whatever the weather, providing vital guidance to erring walkers. This Spanish version is constructed of a huge number of stones of all sorts of shapes and sizes – none of them particularly large. For as each pilgrim walks past, he or she adds another stone, gradually increasing its size each year. Some pilgrims leave stones as a sign of gratitude that they have made it this far, of determination to continue on the route. Some add one in memory of friends and companions who were unable to journey with them, others in tribute to all those who have gone before. And so the cairn continues to grow, topped by a tall, thin, metal cross whose arms stretch spindly into the sky, ethereal after the bulk of the stones at its base.

Waymarks and cairns have been used for thousands of years. They may provide a navigation aid on a difficult route, mark the site of a famous event, indicate a holy place, or simply say, 'I was here'. They come in all sorts of shapes and sizes and have a multitude of meanings.

We too can use cairns in our pilgrimage journey. Small markers, indicators of presences, can act as a reminder to us that this place that is marked is special, holy. It can help us to see a place in a new light, through new eyes. It can start us wondering: 'This particular place, although it seems ordinary, has been singled out as sacred to someone.' Cairns can encourage us to pause and pray, only for a moment, a sentence or two, just enough to ask God's blessing into the place and on the activities that happen there, the people who carry them out.

Cairns in a house are a relatively simple matter, since all you have to do is make sure that they are pleasing to you and do not get in the way of those who live with you. Choose your site with care – it must be sufficiently noticeable that it reminds you to stop and pray, but not so much in the middle of the action that it either becomes a nuisance or is continually being knocked down. You can have more than one cairn; they can mark the significant places of your pilgrimage – your chair, the table. Or you might choose to have just one, perhaps by the front door, to remind you to pray as you enter and leave.

You can make a cairn out of traditional materials – a small pile of pebbles, for example. On a practical note, although polished pebbles look very pretty they are hard to use to build a satisfactory cairn as their smooth surface means that they tend to slide about and not retain the traditional cone shape. However, if four or five smooth pebbles are what seem appropriate for you, then go ahead. Less traditional material can also be used (aim to use objects that are relevant to the place you have chosen to build a cairn), such as a pyramid of eggcups placed next to the kitchen sink. Try not to make the objects too everyday, however, or they will simply be taken up and used!

Building waymarks in a church is a more sensitive matter, as many people use the space. I have found that folding a piece of paper on which a prayer has been written into a pyramid shape and standing it unobtrusively somewhere can cause little offence, although it is necessary to be sensitive.

Out in the community the restrictions are similar – your cairn needs to be made of natural and, ideally, biodegradable materials that blend into the landscape and cause no offence to the other users of the space. All that is necessary is that they appear deliberately made. A small pile of tarmac chippings gathered up from the road can be placed next to the neighbourhood's boundary marker, for example; or assemble a 'tepee' of twigs in a park. Try to use whatever is locally available rather than import material – the aim is to make the cairn look distinctive, not out of place. If you are using material that cannot be built into the classic cairn shape, make the sign of the cross instead. Several of these can be placed along a route that you walk regularly, giving your ordinary journeys added depth as they remind you to see in and through the everyday sights of daily life, opening your eyes to all sorts of wonders.

Reflection

Building a cairn is in itself an act of reflection. Gather the materials slowly and unhurriedly, taking time to look at them and see them properly. Once the cairn is built, try to get into the habit of praying every time you see it – a short sentence will do, or make it longer if you have time. You might want to dedicate each cairn to a different subject or person in your life, so that your daily walk becomes a litany of prayer. Or you might pray more generally, for the people whose lives are affected by the places where you have built cairns.

Acknowledgements and sources of photographs

With grateful thanks to Bishop John Pritchard and Sarah Meyrick, keystones of the Pilgrim Project, and to Andrew Bunch.

Chapter 1 Beginning: © Kate Jewell
http://commons.wikimedia.org/wiki/File:Looking_up_Church_Lane,_Stathern_-_geograph.org.uk_-_64038.jpg

Chapter 2 Prioritizing: Shutterstock © Ersler Dmitry

Chapter 3 Discovering: © Sally Welch

Chapter 4 Struggling: Shutterstock © Brendan Reals

Chapter 5 The Heart of the Matter: © DeeBritt Schultz
http://commons.wikimedia.org/wiki/File:GMHC_2009_Dinner_Table.jpg?uselang=en-gb

Chapter 6 Resting: Shutterstock © cosma

Chapter 7 Remembering: Shutterstock © Mongkol Thonglek

Chapter 8 Beginning Again: Shutterstock © Alex Staroseltsev

Chapter 9 Waymarks and Cairns: © Alan Walker
http://commons.wikimedia.org/wiki/File:Public_footpath_-_geograph.org.uk_-_605944.jpg